the WISDOM *of the*
5 MESSENGERS

To Erin –

Kerry Ottman

KERRY PAUL ALTMAN, PH.D.

the WISDOM *of the* 5 MESSENGERS

LEARNING TO FOLLOW THE
GUIDANCE OF FEELINGS

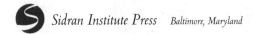 *Sidran Institute Press*   *Baltimore, Maryland*

Note: A number of case studies are offered throughout this book to illustrate the five messengers in real-life settings. While the individuals and situations are based on actual cases, each vignette represents a composite story drawn from cases involving similar issues. I have altered identifying features to preserve client confidentiality, and no case study can be attributed to any single individual or group of individuals. —KPA

Book and cover design by Kachergis Book Design of Pittsboro, North Carolina.

13 12 11 10 09 08 07   8 7 6 5 4 3 2 1

Library of Congress Cataloging-in-Publication Data
Altman, Kerry Paul, 1951–
    The wisdom of the five messengers : learning to follow the guidance of feelings / Kerry Paul Altman.
        p. cm.
    Includes bibliographical references.
    ISBN-13: 978-1-886968-19-6 (alk. paper)
    ISBN-10: 1-886968-19-5 (alk. paper)
    1. Emotions.   I. Title.
BF561.A485 2007
152.4—dc22

                            2007033536

This book is dedicated to

Nan, Lana, and Zach

for all they have taught me

about the Five Messengers

CONTENTS

the WISDOM *of the*
5 MESSENGERS

INTRODUCING THE
FIVE MESSENGERS

Our feelings are our most genuine paths to knowledge.
—Audre Lorde

When the inspiration for this book first came to me, my original idea for a title was *The Wisdom of the Five Angels* because it conveyed the quality of grace that is an important part of us listening to ourselves. A trusted friend and colleague dissuaded me from using it for this book, however, saying: "People who buy books about angels are the last people who are going to want to read the book you want to write. You want to attract readers who are willing to pay attention to the messages that come from within, not those who are looking for some miraculous intervention from outside themselves."

I took his criticism to heart, though I regret that the present title does not adequately convey the "angelic" beauty and serenity of the five messengers. While this is not a religious book, it is, ultimately, a spiritual one. It deals with the very thing that makes us who we are—the human spirit, made tangible to us through the five emotions: anger, sadness, fear, happiness, and love.

I have worked as a clinical psychologist for the past twenty-five years in settings as disparate as the locked wards of a federal psychiatric hospital and a suburban private practice. I have had the honor of helping clients through a range of emotional maladies, from relatively uncomplicated reactions to life's challenges to the most complex psychological issues imaginable. Regardless

INTRODUCING *the* FIVE MESSENGERS

of the particular stressor that brings a person to seek treatment, what psychotherapy has to offer is really quite simple. It is a process of helping an individual acknowledge, understand, and accept his or her feelings, then find the courage to use those feelings as guides to making fulfilling choices.

Yet, despite this simple explanation of the practical value of psychotherapy, the process of achieving peace of mind is anything but simple. Often there are formidable blocks—borne of internalized messages and misconceptions—to an easy and natural relationship with feelings. These blocks sometimes pit one feeling against another, complicate the emotional experience, and cloud what should be a clear and unfettered pathway from the senses to the heart. When allowed to flow more freely, feelings are ultimately messengers that travel from the realm of experience to our consciousness to inform and guide us. The messengers are always with us and will never abandon us; from birth to death they are as close to us as our heartbeat and our breath. They are not demanding, though they hate to be ignored, and they will go to great lengths to make their presence known.

Through my own journey and in supporting the work and growth of my clients, I have come to realize that there is a lot of misunderstanding and erroneous expectation where feelings are concerned. Much of this derives from our most personal experiences and, to some degree, prevailing cultural values that lead us to believe some feelings are "good" while others are "bad." By extension, we often judge feelings as right or wrong, acceptable or unacceptable, OK or not OK. When we subject our feelings to this critical judgment, we find ways to edit or deflect the messages that we have trouble with by attempting to kill the messenger to avoid the presence of the unwanted feeling. But unlike Shakespeare's Rosencrantz and Guildenstern, the messengers cannot be destroyed. In fact, despite our profoundly creative efforts to drive them away, the messengers will always reveal themselves in one form or another, pleading for recognition and acceptance.

This book presents a judgment-free exploration of the five

messengers. I offer the reader my perspective on what each of the five primary feelings is truly about, with the hope of instilling an appreciation of each emotion as a normal human response to the situations we face throughout our lives. It is only when we can see and experience our feelings for what they are, rather than what we want or do not want them to be, that we can begin to value their true calling as messengers. If they are anything at all, the five emotions are indeed messengers, carrying the most important messages to our consciousness, along with the only true opportunity for free choice.

The Wisdom of the Five Messengers also addresses the nature of the messages that the feelings invite us to attend to and explores some of the many ways in which we can begin to listen and respond more immediately and directly to the guidance they offer.

Obviously, this is not the first book to address the realm of emotion. The world of feelings has been the purview of social scientists for hundreds of years and the muse of poets for much longer than that. Some have written of just four emotions as primary, considering love to be more akin to a particular form of happiness than a pure emotion in and of itself. Others have included such emotional states as guilt, shame, excitement, and lust as unique feelings unto themselves. I will try to help the reader appreciate how simultaneous or conflicting feelings may create emotional confusion, and how the feelings can be distilled to their more basic forms so that their messages, wisdom, and guidance can be more clearly seen.

The ability to regard emotions as messengers and as guides is only partly a matter of will. From the onset of an experience, feelings often travel a circuitous route before they reach our conscious minds. They flow through a process of evaluation based on past experience and old messages about what the feeling means and whether or not it should be allowed. Before looking at the five feelings themselves, I discuss the obstacles that make acceptance of our true nature more difficult than it should be.

Ultimately, I suppose, this is a book about truth. It is not about any particular truth, however; it is about your truth and my truth, which can be known solely in the most personal and subjective way. It is the truth that is influenced by our families, our teachers, our cultures, and our experiences, but they can never define it. It is the truth that is available to each person who is willing and able to listen, without judgment, to the emotions that flow in natural response to the world around us. Attending to these emotions and heeding the messages they try to deliver is the one true road to peace of mind.

1.

THE HUMAN FUSE BOX

We're gonna vent our frustration
If we don't, we're gonna blow a 50-amp fuse.
  —The Rolling Stones, "You Can't Always Get
  What You Want"

To help you understand the role of feelings in the overall scheme of the human system, I offer this metaphor. In a crudely poetic way, the human being can be likened to a house.

Even though certain characteristics are common to all houses, each house, like each person, is composed of a unique combination of appearance, style, and features that sets it apart from all others. Every house has a physical structure—a basic form and outer shell—that is analogous to the human body. The wiring that runs throughout the house corresponds to the central nervous system; the electricity that runs through the wires equates to stress.

In every home, some amount of electrical current is always flowing through the wires to maintain such basic functions as keeping the refrigerator or clocks running. In the human "house," some amount of stress is necessary at all times to allow people to perform such basic tasks as getting out of bed in the morning or brushing their teeth. People tend to think of stress as a bad or an undesirable thing, but this is largely the result of semantics and popular misuse of the word. When people talk about being "stressed out," they are actually referring to a feeling of system overload, which will be discussed in a moment. Stress in the human system is neither good nor bad; it is simply the energy that keeps things running and moves things along.

So far so good. But everyone knows what happens when too many appliances run at one time or when one appliance demands too much current for the electrical system to handle, or if a sudden, unexpected bolt of lightning hits the house and overloads the circuitry. When the electrical surge overloads the circuitry, a safety mechanism kicks into place to prevent a catastrophe. The appropriate circuit breaker switches off, shutting down the overloaded circuit until the problem can be addressed. Or, in old-fashioned terms and popular parlance, the system blows a fuse.

In human terms, a similar process takes place. Our physiology is designed to handle a fair amount of stress, although individual capacities for dealing with stress or a particular kind of stress vary greatly. Even the strongest or the smartest or the most emotionally aware people may experience more stress than they can handle, however; at that point their safety mechanism kicks in and they blow a fuse.

Everyone is aware of the physical safety valves, or fuses, that tend to blow when the human system is overloaded. Migraine headaches, lower back pain, stomach ailments, and numerous other aches, pains, and physical discomforts are often triggered in response to high levels of stress. These physical symptoms call our attention to the fact that the level of stress we are experiencing has begun to tax our capacities to manage or deal with it. Perhaps, like the house circuit that is running too many appliances at one time, the individual is trying to perform too many tasks at once, spreading personal resources too thin. Or, like the single large appliance that uses too much electricity, a person may be taking on a task for which he or she lacks the appropriate skills or training—a task that is simply too difficult to deal with. Or sometimes, like the unexpected bolt of lightning, an unforeseen event occurs which puts a sudden, overwhelming demand on an individual, presenting a situation that the person is unprepared for or unequipped to handle.

It is easy to recognize the physical reactions to stress when they arise: headaches flair, backs go out, stomachs ache, directing us—at times *forcing* us—to pay attention to the way we are managing the level of stress in our lives. It is more difficult to recognize and acknowledge the emotional response that accompanies a stressful or difficult situation. Whether we are engaged in a wonderful and carefree experience or embroiled in a difficult challenge, our feelings are always with us. One or more of the five emotions—anger, sadness, fear, happiness, and love—is close at hand in every moment. These emotions also serve as fuses in the human house, and so finely tuned are these emotional fuses that attending to them can allow us to adjust and make choices long before a circuit blows.

Each of the emotions will be discussed in greater detail in subsequent chapters, but I will use a firsthand example of the emotion fear to illustrate its value as a fuse in the human circuit. Fear is a member of the "Vigilant Triad" of emotions. Along with anger and sadness, it is often erroneously regarded as a "bad" feeling, though this is an unfortunate and potentially tragic way of looking at it. It is at times less desirable and more challenging than other emotions, but it is no more "bad" than happiness is "good." Fear is simply a normal human response to a perceived threat. If its presence is acknowledged and its message is attended to early enough, we can make choices to address the perceived threat and avoid the possibility of simple, ordinary fear escalating into an overwhelming experience of terror.

My wife and I recently attended a Saturday night wedding at a local hotel. The parking garage was so crowded that we had to park in a fairly remote section of the underground complex.

After the ceremony and before the dinner, we walked back to the car to retrieve a cell phone we had left behind. We exited the elevator on the wrong level and were about to walk back up to where our car was parked when, halfway up the ramp, we saw two men dumping water from a cooler they had removed from the bed of their pickup truck. They were dressed in hunting or fishing clothes and had clearly been drinking. One of them started singing in an overly loud voice when he saw us. My wife took my hand and began directing me back to the elevator.

"What's wrong?" I asked.

"Those guys are making me uncomfortable; let's just take the elevator up to our level," she replied. Which is what we did.

My personal radar had not been alerted by the actions of the two men, and of course they may just have been two "good ol' boys" with no ill intent. My wife is no shrinking violet and is not usually intimidated or frightened easily, but for some reason, she experienced a degree of fear that had risen to the level of discomfort. In its role as messenger, fear had alerted my wife to her perception of a potential unknown threat and had invited her to respond. She listened to the message and responded quickly and appropriately, and we returned to the party without giving the minor incident a second thought. The fear fuse flared up slightly, but perceptibly, and by attending to it the circuit was restored to a healthy balance.

I offer this personal anecdote as a small example of the ordinary and everyday function of feelings as fuses. In the context of an entire day, week, or lifetime, the incident I described is an easily forgotten event. But what might the consequences have been had my wife ignored her feeling and not attended to the invitation of the messenger to respond in some way? The likelihood of an actual physical attack seems remote, but many rapes and assaults do take place in secluded parking structures. At the very least, an uncomfortable and anxious walk up the ramp past the men was avoided. The stress that would have accompanied that anxious walk would have taken some time to dissipate, affecting my wife's ability to fully enjoy the party. By listening to the message presented by her own emotions, she made a reasoned choice to address the situation in the way that made the most sense to her, and it worked out just fine.

This autopsy of a small incident may seem absurdly overanalytical, but it illustrates a very critical point regarding the relationship between all people and their feelings. It is precisely the small incidents that form the foundation of our ability to attend to feelings and the messages they provide. It often seems easier to avoid feelings and focus on a task or goal. Indeed, taking the ramp would have been the shorter route to the car and may have saved us thirty seconds or so. But when we begin the process of ignoring feelings for short-term gain, we lose sight of their role as fuses in the human circuitry, and their ultimate value as messengers and guides drifts further and further away from our consciousness. We begin to regard feelings as something to be ignored or overcome in our search for tangible rewards, which is the beginning of a quest without end. Sadly, this notion of feelings as an obstacle to our desires frequently begins with the messages of childhood, which makes the relearning process all the more difficult.

Let's return for a moment to the house analogy. Anyone who has lived in an old house with an actual fuse box rather than a circuit breaker may be aware of the penny trick. When an electrical circuit overloads and a fuse blows, the fuse must be replaced before the electric circuit is restored. When a new fuse isn't immediately available, you can unscrew the fuse, place a penny behind it, and screw it back into place. The copper penny conducts electricity, essentially avoiding the fuse and completing the circuit. This is only a short-term and potentially dangerous solution to the problem, however, since the jerry-rigged circuit now lacks a safety valve. If an electrical overload should occur, a resultant fire could burn down the entire house.

Human beings are just as creative where the human fuse box is concerned, inventing all kinds of ways to put the penny behind the fuse. Substance abuse, sex addictions, obsessive overworking, and extreme diets or exercise programs are but a few of the ways people try to avoid looking at the real issues that beg attention. Our feelings offer us the opportunity to assess our interface with the world around us, to know what is going well and to become more aware of the things that are not going well. In their role as messengers, feelings can point us to the trouble spots and alert us to things in our life that need attention or correction, but they do not guarantee that change will be easy. In fact, since all change requires an honest assessment of a situation and a commitment to doing things differently, change is often quite difficult and at times painful. This can lead to an avoidance of feelings in an effort to evade the discomfort of making a difficult choice. To accomplish this, people put the penny behind the fuse and keep on going, requiring more and more energy to avoid the persistent messengers and essentially condemning themselves to a restless unhappiness.

We can spend a lifetime running from feelings, based upon the faulty view that emotional discomfort is a bad thing and should be avoided if at all possible. But perhaps the saddest part of the story is the relationship that never materializes. An honest relationship with our feelings can provide us with a vehicle for truly appreciating the personal connection between our worlds and our selves, giving us the opportunity to make mindful choices and to experience full ownership of our lives. The more we acknowledge, trust, and value our feelings, the more aware we will be of the intimate connection between us and our surroundings. This connection is at times a joyful experience and at times a painful intimacy, but it is always our personal truth.

Nonetheless, pain is painful. In order to avoid pain many of us have learned to view feelings as the enemy, as something to keep at a distance, to be managed and controlled. This is a tragic and ultimately impossible task, for while feelings can be held at bay indefinitely, the energy required to do so will ultimately create the bars of a person's own prison. Feelings may be difficult, at times excruciatingly so, but they are never the enemy. In truth, feelings are the best friends any of us will ever know.

THE VIGILANT
TRIAD

*Keep your heart with all vigilance, for from it flow
the springs of life.*
—Proverbs 4:23

*A*ny discussion of the vigilant triad must first address the notions of good feelings vs. bad feelings. Anger, sadness, and fear are all primarily protec-
tive in nature, and the guidance they offer addresses
the realm of safety and security. Yet, ironically, they are
frequently referred to as "bad" feelings. This is not only
a disrespectful view of the important role these messengers play but also a potentially unsafe attitude. True,
the feelings of the vigilant triad are often associated
with painful and difficult life events, but it is important
that we understand the distinction between feeling bad
and bad feeling.

Feeling bad is a statement about the difficulty or
unpleasantness of an emotional state; *bad feeling* is a
critical judgment of an emotional state and implies that

the feeling is not in our best interest. We tend to avoid or dismiss things we consider bad for us, but taking this approach to the vigilant triad leaves us vulnerable and unprepared for the inevitable difficulties that are a part of life. A healthy relationship with the messengers anger, sadness, and fear is always in our best interest.

Anger, sadness, and fear represent normal human responses to injustice, loss, and uncertainty. They appear in response to life circumstances that stimulate these concerns and are vigilant in that they are available to guide us toward the best possible choices to avoid unnecessary pain. Although anger, sadness, and fear are not an *antidote* to pain, they can lead people to respond promptly to perceptions of threat or hurt and to maintain a watchful eye as they move through the course of a difficult situation.

The vigilant triad is often thought of in extreme forms, which distorts the feelings' more typical appearances and minimizes their value as messengers and guides. Anger, sadness, and fear are not the same thing as aggression, despair, and terror, but the tendency to make these associations contributes to the difficulty we have in learning to appreciate and value the wisdom of these messengers. They are often seen as character flaws rather than the important and vital aspects of character they truly are.

To some degree, the vigilant triad has its roots in the most primitive aspects of our animal nature, but the messages the feelings invite us to consider influence the choices we make in every aspect of modern life. The lessons of childhood and other life experiences play a critical role in shaping our ability to attend to these feelings, and our capacity to benefit from their wisdom and guidance is shaped by these early influences. Often misunderstood, the messengers of the vigilant triad are maligned when they should be admired and avoided when they should be listened to. Our emotional health and sense of balance require us to do whatever we can to embrace every opportunity to forge a healthy relationship with the messengers of the vigilant triad, but before we can accomplish this we must understand and appreciate the nature and intention of each of the messengers. Stimulating the reader's thoughts in this regard is the aim of the next three chapters: "Anger: The Messenger of Injustice," "Sadness: The Messenger of Loss," and "Fear: The Messenger of the Unknown."

2.

ANGER

THE MESSENGER OF INJUSTICE

If you are patient in one moment of anger, you will escape a hundred days of sorrow.

—Chinese Proverb

THE PHYSIOLOGY OF ANGER

Poor anger. Civilization has played a cruel trick on this courageous messenger, causing it to be widely and falsely regarded as the least desirable of all emotions, though it is merely the most misunderstood. Because anger is often the emotional precursor to aggressive or violent behavior it is wrongly viewed as a destructive or dangerous feeling, an emotion to be avoided, ignored, or denied. As with all of the emotions, however, such efforts are ultimately futile, and anger will do whatever it can to be recognized and attended to.

Our most primitive responses to the possibility of threat have long been conceptualized as a function of the "flight-fight" mechanism of the brain. It is easy to see how an efficient assessment of a potentially dangerous situation would be essential for survival in the animal kingdom. It is generally believed that the perception of a potential threat stimulates a part of the brain called the amygdala. This triggers the hypothalamus, which stimulates an automatic response to the danger. When the danger is perceived as something that cannot be avoided and must be defended against, the sympathetic nervous system stimulates the release of adrenaline. This state is accompanied by an increase in heart rate and blood pressure, muscle tension, rapid shallow breathing, and a general readiness to stand and fight the perceived threat.

Our experience of the complex physiological responses that precede the fight against the invasive threat has been given the name anger. This brief discussion of the primitive nature of the fight side of the flight-fight mechanism may conjure up images of cavemen defending their families from attacking beasts, or warriors boldly repelling an attack from a hostile clan. From this perspective, it is clear that anger is a valuable and necessary internal system for summoning up courage. It is a messenger that warns of a disruptive and potentially lethal intrusion and pushes ordinary human beings to heroic action. It is considerably more difficult to see the value of anger when a minor traffic altercation ends in a senseless violent tragedy because of the inappropriate expression of the messenger.

LEARNING ABOUT ANGER

Anger is a normal human emotional response to the perception of injustice. Like all feelings, anger is experienced along a continuum, which ranges from barely noticeable to extreme depending upon the event that stimulates the emotion. On the barely noticeable side is the mild frustration that accompanies an event such as trying to open a stubborn mayonnaise jar. On the extreme side of the spectrum is the furious response that might follow an act of betrayal. There is no absolute standard and no formula to determine how much anger is appropriate for a particular situation. The *perception* of injustice plays a major role in the processing of anger, and perception is a variable, subjective experience. One person may respond to a minor traffic altercation with a shake of the head or a moment of annoyance that quickly dissipates, while another person might see the incident as a major violation worthy of physical attack. One need only attend a youth soccer game to see the apoplectic reaction to a questionable call by the referee of some red-faced parent on the sideline, while other parents—and usually the players themselves—shrug off the incident and get on with enjoying the game.

So what accounts for these widely divergent expressions of anger? To answer this question we must look at the relationship people have with anger, and we must appreciate the common misconceptions and false beliefs people hold about this powerfully experienced emotional state. Of all the messengers, anger is the one most often regarded as a "bad" emotion. At a very young age, we are taught to have little respect for anger, and we are rarely guided to a healthy and intimate relationship with the feeling.

In families where anger is followed almost immediately with yelling, shaming, hitting, or other forms of intimidation, children never really have the opportunity to learn about anger as a valuable emotion. The aggressiveness of a bigger and stronger individual with total control over all aspects of the child's life leaves little room for anything other than a fearful response. The child gets the clear message that anger and aggression are one and the same and are to be avoided if at all possible. A healthy discussion of anger and its many possible avenues of expression never takes place in such settings. Consequently, children may come to believe that aggressive behavior is the only way anger can be expressed; the long-term implications of this faulty belief can have a serious impact upon later functioning in adult life.

Adults who were raised in aggressive or violent settings often take one of two paths in their relationship with anger in adult life. The unpleasantness of their experience of aggression may lead them to avoid or deny anger, which leaves them ill-prepared for dealing with the minor injustices of everyday life. They push away the messenger at every turn, unable to give credence to their own experience, which paves the way for expression of the feeling in indirect and often self-defeating ways.

Some years ago I led an outpatient psychotherapy group for

adult survivors of childhood abuse. One member of the group, who had been diagnosed with depression and posttraumatic symptoms, offered this concise and eloquent description of the "stuck" feeling many survivors of abusive families report: "My problem is that I'm angry about being so afraid all the time, but I'm afraid of my anger."

The other common path of individuals who were raised in aggressive or violent settings is the re-creation of the behavior they despised as a child. These adults respond aggressively, at times violently, to any perceived injustice, and they are similarly unable to listen to the messages of anger and the invitation to consider options. It is as if such individuals have only one tool in their toolbox and are unaware of the value of any other tool. The lesson learned in childhood was that aggression is the only, indeed the "proper," expression of anger.

Several psychological models have been offered to explain this way of acting, focusing on early learning, role development, and the notion of identification with the aggressive parent figure. Even adults who hated the violence they experienced in childhood may incorporate the aggressive response to anger as a primary aspect of their identity. For such individuals, aggression is not just how they behave in response to the feeling of anger; aggression becomes an important part of how they see themselves. "I don't take shit from anyone" becomes the mantra of people with this self-view, and their tendency is to do battle with every perceived injustice. They see "shit" everywhere, and they seem unable to avoid stepping in it.

It is not just wildly angry and aggressive families that teach their children faulty lessons about anger, however. The most loving and nurturing parents often teach children to regard anger as an emotion to be avoided or denied. Take the example of a simple sandbox tussle over a cherished dump truck that one child has taken away from another. Parents will typically separate the children, soothe their cries, and attempt to encourage a peaceful resolution to the fight with statements about the importance of sharing and a brokered deal for playing with the toy. Although this is an appropriate and effective response to a minor crisis, an important opportunity has slipped by.

By focusing exclusively on resolving the altercation and restoring peace, parents miss the chance to help the child in the emerging relationship with his or her own emotions. Perhaps the parent could talk to the child about what the child is feeling and how he or she behaved. This would validate the feeling while teaching an important lesson about the difference between feelings and behavior. Something as simple as, "It's OK to feel angry when you don't get to play with the toy, but it's not OK to throw sand at Billy when you feel that way," can introduce the notion that anger is not the enemy.

A follow-up conversation about other ways to respond to anger could be of further benefit. The parent could list some of the many options for the child: "We can take the truck and go home where no one can compete for the toy. We can take turns playing with it. We can throw the toy away or cut it in half." The spirit of such a conversation would not be to abdicate parental responsibility and leave it up to the child; rather, it is a way of helping the child begin to see anger as a messenger. In this case it is a messenger of the perceived injustice involving the coveted dump truck, but, more important, it is a messenger of the notion of choice in response to the injustice.

At this point I can imagine readers rolling their eyes and saying: "Who has time for all of that? Do you need to be Sigmund Freud to take your kid to the park?" So, let me temper my comments with the assurance that an analytic approach to parenting would be little fun for parent or child and would completely miss out on the important lesson that emotions are *experiences,* not concepts. The point I am trying to make is simply that our earliest and most ordinary of interactions with caregivers may predispose us toward a lack of respect for anger and may set the stage for the unfortunate view of anger as a bad and unnecessary emotion.

THE HISTORY OF SOCIETY IN TWO MINUTES OR LESS

In primitive times, the value of anger as a messenger was clear and unambiguous. Anything that threatened the security of the individual was quickly perceived through the senses, stimulating a rapid assessment of the danger. If the threat was perceived as overwhelming and avoidable, the flight-fight mechanism triggered the fear response and the fear messenger said, loudly and clearly, "Get out of here, now!" If the threat was perceived as conquerable or unavoidable, the same mechanism triggered the anger response, and the anger messenger said, "Stand and do battle," or "Attack." If you had the resources to heed the messenger's advice, you lived. If you didn't, you suffered or died. Threat and injustice were synonymous.

For the greater benefit of the species, cooperation was required, which led to the development of rules, laws, and government. The shared benefits of society were accompanied by the shared responsibilities of social living. Living became less primitive, and more sophistication was required if someone was to thrive in a community of others. Since emotions represent the meeting point of perception and experience, the realm of feelings became more and more sophisticated to meet the variety and subtlety of a growing and evolving society.

Living in a social community requires a different relationship with anger from the primitive flight-fight response. Threat and injustice are universally perceived in many situations, but the everyday experience of these concepts is a relative thing. Applying the law of the jungle to the perceived injustice of a child forgetting to do a household chore would be an outrageous overreaction, to say the least. Fortunately, society has instituted laws and regulations to attempt to harness excessively aggressive responses to angry feelings.

Unfortunately, the lessons we teach and learn about anger often perpetuate the view of it as a primitive and aggressive emotion that has no place in a civilized society. This misconception can always be traced to the pairing of the emotion of anger with aggressive behavior. Anger is a feeling, not a behavior, but it is often perceived through the lens of the aggressive and violent behaviors that sometimes follow the emotional experience. Don't take my word for it. Type the word *anger* into an Internet search engine and take a look at the hundreds of references that appear. With only occasional exception, the references describe anger as a "destructive" emotion, a "problem," or something to be purged from the psyche. Even the common use of the term "anger management" is an unfortunate misnomer, for while anger management groups have helped thousands of individuals learn to monitor and control their aggressive behavior, it is not anger that is actually managed. Aggressive responses to angry feelings need to be checked, monitored, and managed. Anger needs to be listened to.

IN PRAISE OF ANGER

Let me pause here to give anger its due respect. Anger has played an important role, perhaps the most critical role, in every meaningful development in the history of humankind. Before recorded time, someone got frustrated about having to lug a pile of wood across a field or up a hill, sparking the idea that led to the invention of the wheel. Anger about the injustices of working conditions led to the labor reforms of the 1920s and '30s, just as anger about the injustice of racism led to the civil rights movement in the 1960s. Advances in medicine, technology, and social conditions can all be seen as responses to frustration and a sense of unfairness about the prevailing circumstances. While it is true that aggressive and violent encounters among individuals, groups, and nations have often followed the experience of anger, the pairing of anger with aggressive behavior is a limited, one-dimensional view of what anger is and the possibilities it seeks to inform us about.

Unfortunately, the messages of childhood are deeply ingrained, particularly where anger is concerned. The pairing of the emotion anger with the notion of aggressive behavior teaches us either to fear and avoid the emotion or to regard it as an unrealistically powerful vehicle for addressing anything that is not going our way. Social and religious institutions often regard anger as a bad or sinful emotion, wrongly teaching that love and kindness are the opposite of anger. These deeply held notions make it difficult for individuals to open up to new ways of regarding anger and to listen to the personal messages their anger has to offer. Fortunately, a sincere desire to try a new relationship with anger is the only thing required to begin the transformation.

In order to hear the messages offered by our anger, we have to be willing and able to listen to it, and in order to listen to anger, we have to learn to put space between our experience of anger and our reaction to it. Aggressive and violent reactions to anger are often immediate, knee-jerk responses to the perceived injustice. But many other behavioral responses are similarly unconscious, spaceless reactions to angry feelings. Anxiety, panic, somatic symptoms, and often depression are common ways in which anger expresses itself when space between the feeling and the reaction to it has not been cultivated.

Alice

A former client of mine, whom I will call Alice, initially sought treatment to address an onset of recurring panic attacks. After numerous medical tests and several trips to the hospital emergency room with feared, but nonexistent, heart attacks, the client reluctantly came to see me at the urging of her family physician. Antianxiety medication had been prescribed but offered only minimal relief, and Alice's panic attacks—or fear of unexpected ones—were beginning to impinge on all aspects of her life. She was an attractive woman in her mid-30s who worked in a middle management position for a consulting firm and was raising a sixteen-year-old son alone.

The first several sessions focused on helping Alice find some relief from the symptoms that were threatening to overrun her life. She responded well to some education about the psychological nature of panic attacks and the reassurance that they always pass and are never fatal. She diligently practiced at home the relaxation exercises we worked on in sessions. In a relatively short span of time, Alice had achieved the symptom relief she wanted.

What she had not achieved, however, was an understanding of what was causing the panic attacks in the first place, nor had she developed the process needed to avoid overwhelming panic in the future. Panic-prone clients always overvalue control, and they often reject the notion that factors outside their everyday awareness predispose them to panic episodes. They tend to end therapy prematurely, as soon as they achieve a brief period of freedom from the intrusive symptoms, though they often return to treatment after being blindsided by another panic attack down the road. Because Alice had achieved several weeks without panic attacks, I expected her to end therapy without a deeper understanding of her issues, but at what I had assumed would be our final session, she surprised me by saying, "Well, now that I don't have to worry about anxiety, I realize that my life sucks."

When her husband left her with a young child and very few resources, Alice took stock of her life and set a determined course to assure her son's safety and security. Without family or friends to rely on, she got a good job, sent her son to good schools, supported his interests and activities, and generally devoted herself to his welfare and happiness. Her first full-blown panic attack came while her son was attending a two-week residential basketball camp. Over the previous year or two, he had begun to show normal and healthy signs of independence, but his attendance at the camp marked the first time in a decade that Alice felt utterly without focus or purpose. She was uncertain about what to do, feeling oddly lost and undefined, which led to the panic attacks. It was not the event itself that caused Alice's panic attacks; rather, her inability to recognize and listen to her anger led to her extreme discomfort and the fear that she was losing her grip on reality.

Alice was raised in a household where angry feelings were rarely acknowledged or expressed. Her father was the "strong, silent type," and her mother valued cheerfulness over all other emotional states. Alice was an excellent student and athlete and there was little conflict in the home. When Alice was just entering her teen years, however, her father shattered the Norman Rockwell image by announcing that he was leaving the family for another woman with an established family of her own. Alice's mother dissolved into depression and her father distanced himself as much as possible. Fearful of driving her mother and father even further away from her by expressing her own feelings, Alice applied herself to school, then to work, then to her own marriage, then to raising her son on her own. She put her nose to the grindstone and did not lift it up until the panic attacks left her no other choice but to attend to the feelings she had long ignored.

In the course of therapy, Alice began to acknowledge the anger that had been with her all along—the normal human response to the series of personal injustices she had long endured. While she was sad about her son's independence and fearful about her own future, Alice was primarily angry about her increasingly joyless life. Her son's healthy individuation underscored the bleak facts of her own life: she had few friends, no substantial family relationships, an unsatisfying job, and no passions or outside interests.

Once she learned to recognize and express her own anger, Alice began to see that she had denied angry feelings since childhood. She had developed personal clichés and little sound bites to deflect questions about her parents' divorce, her father's abandonment of the family, her mother's depression. When asked about her own feelings, Alice would say something like: "That's their issue, not mine," or "I had a great family life for fourteen years; that's more than most kids get, right?" Healthy expression of anger was neither modeled nor valued in her family and was discouraged by default. The notion that anger is not only OK but also a normal and healthy emotion came as a revelation to Alice. She began to tentatively explore her own feelings about past and present circumstances and forged a solid relationship with anger, appreciating its value as a messenger.

She listened to the anger she felt about being alone yet again and heard the message loud and clear: *You are lonely and need to do something about that.* She reconnected with old friends, joined an adult indoor soccer team, and started accepting some of the requests for dates she had always declined.

She listened more deeply and heard other messages: *You protect your parents' feelings and deny your own. You want a better relationship with them and need to discuss this with them.* Alice made a sincere effort to talk to her parents about the past hurts and the emotional distance from her they had maintained since the divorce. She started a dialog with her father, which led to a more satisfying and surprisingly supportive relationship. Alice's mother, on the other hand, refused to discuss the past and avoided any discussion of her daughter's feelings. While Alice's efforts did not lead to the emotional reunion with her mother she had fantasized, Alice did come away with a realistic view of her mother's limitations which helped her let go of her own unrealistic expectations.

When Alice ended treatment with me she was not problem free. No one ever is. She did not leave with the assurance that she would never again face loneliness, disappointment, rejection, or pain. No such assurance is offered in life. What Alice did gain was nonetheless what she had come for: relief from the panic attacks, which came with her willingness to experience and attend to her own feelings more directly. She stopped avoiding uncomfortable feelings, specifically anger, and learned to make personal choices by following her anger's wisdom and guidance.

I present the preceding case study neither to promote psychotherapy nor to suggest that it is the only road to emotional wisdom. Psychotherapy can provide the professional expertise and guidance some individuals need to sort out their emotional issues, but it is not the psychotherapy per se that brings about the change. Change comes from the ability to listen, without judgment, to one's emotional truth and to make personal choices based on that truth. In Alice's case, the therapy setting provided her with the opportunity to develop the space between her experience of the world and her reaction to it, giving her the chance to truly exercise choice over her destiny.

LISTENING TO ANGER

Listening to feelings and cultivating a nonreactive relationship with them require three things: desire, new learning, and practice. Some guidelines and suggestions for this process will be offered later in this book, but for now let's specifically take a look at how someone might develop his or her relationship with anger. If there is a sincere interest in improving a relationship with anger, there is always ample opportunity to practice. Situations that evoke the emotion of anger are everywhere: the annoying telemarketer's phone call at dinner time or the rude salesperson or the insensitive remark from a spouse, friend, or child. Such everyday injustices elicit anger and thus offer the opportunity to work on the relationship with the emotion.

Working on the relationship with anger as situations evoke the feeling is a little bit like learning to swim by jumping into the deep end of the pool. A more controlled situation usually provides a better opportunity for new learning; in the case of anger, this can best be achieved by seeking out opportunities to experience it rather than waiting for them to appear. On the surface this may sound a little strange, since the notion of intentionally looking for anger cuts right to the heart of our deeply held notions of anger as a bad emotion. But if there is a wish to learn about something, then we must seek out opportunities to become educated.

Taking this approach to anger is actually a very simple thing to do. One would be hard-pressed to read any newspaper or to surf through TV channels for more than five minutes without finding some story that evokes anger. A walk through one's neighborhood can lead to finding trash that someone has carelessly thrown on the ground, or dog poop that someone has failed to clean up. Upon finding the anger, one should take the time to recognize it and become familiar with it. Do not ignore it or judge it or run from it. Name it and claim it as a righteous feeling.

Once anger has been acknowledged and accepted, a person can begin to hear its messages by asking a few focusing questions. "What is the injustice I perceive? What makes it unjust? Would this be universally perceived as an injustice, or is it something personal and unique to my experience of things?" The next question is the most precious of all, for its answer is always the most personal and most important message the feeling has to offer: "What do I choose to do about this injustice?"

The answer to the question of action requires an assessment of the consequences. Something as simple as the anger evoked by seeing the trash on the side of the road can lead to numerous possible responses, each with its own consequences. Picking up the trash might make one feel neighborly, but resentful of the person who made the mess. Leaving the trash on the road is another option, but it might be unsatisfying because the visual annoyance remains.

Where anger is concerned, residual emotion is often part of the consequence whether someone chooses to act or not to act, and the issue becomes one of making the choice whose consequences, however unsatisfying, one is most willing to accept. Such consideration may be extremely difficult and painful, as in the case of the anger related to personal experiences of abuse as a child. This is also the case with the choices we make to deal with such social injustices as racism, world hunger, or any other large-scale concern. Whether we take on the issue as a crusader or choose to ignore it entirely, anger invites us to consider the potential consequences of our choices. While we are not required to accept the invitation, it is always in our best interest to listen carefully to the messages regarding our choices, since choice is the foundation of our destiny.

WHAT IT IS, WHAT IT IS NOT

Anger is not violence. Anger is not destructive. It is not wrong or bad or evil or sinful. Anger is human nature's way of alerting us to something we perceive as amiss and unfair. It is a messenger that seeks to inform us of injustice as we experience it, and it invites us to consider the options available to us to set things right. When a person's anger causes personal or interpersonal problems, some outside assistance might be necessary, but ultimately, a person's well-being does not come from a therapist or any other outside force. It comes from making the choices that we perceive to be in our best interest, which can best be assessed through a clear and honest appraisal of the circumstances we face and the options available to us. Where anger is concerned, this essential honesty can be achieved only when we reject simplistic negative notions of this important feeling and regard the emotion as a valued messenger and guide.

SADNESS

THE MESSENGER OF LOSS

Our sweetest songs are those that tell of saddest thought.
—Percy Bysshe Shelley

Where would we be without sadness? Of all the messengers, sadness is the only one whose appearance is absolutely guaranteed at some point in life. It is an absurd notion, but one could theoretically go through life without encountering situations that would stimulate the appearance of anger, fear, happiness, or love, but sadness is a response to something no one can ultimately avoid: the experience of loss.

THE CHEMICAL MECHANICS OF SADNESS

In researching this section of the chapter, I had a very hard time finding a concise explanation of the physiology of sadness. The first difficulty I encountered was the distinction between normal sadness and depression. Researchers and writers agree that the two are different, but from a strictly biological perspective the difference is generally regarded as a matter of degree. The distinction between sadness and depression will be explored in a moment, but their shared biology deserves some discussion.

When we perceive we have lost something of value, a process of slowing down and regrouping takes place. The chemical transfer of messages throughout the brain's nerve cells begins to slow down as the neurotransmitters that carry the messages from one neuron to the next become less efficient in doing their job. The substructure of the brain that regulates emotions, known as the limbic system, is affected in a manner that may stimulate the release of hormones believed to be associated with sadness and depression.

This brings me to the second difficulty I encountered in trying to offer a brief explanation of the physiology of sadness. While we know a great deal about the symptoms and behaviors associated with sadness and depression, we have no biological litmus test to measure these emotional states. Our understanding of how neurotransmitters are related to depression is not completely clear, and it is based largely on studies involving antidepressant medications. Hormone studies have been similarly inconclusive. For example, individuals with a diagnosis of clinical depression often have an increased level of a hormone called cortisone, but this is true for only about half of diagnosed individuals.

Research is ongoing and may yield a clearer biochemical picture some day, but it does seem clear that the perception of loss stimulates a complex physiological mechanism. Some perceived losses are unique to the individual, while other losses may be universally perceived as such. The emotional experience of the change that takes place when we perceive a loss has been given the name sadness.

SADNESS AND DEPRESSION

The continuum of sadness ranges from a mild sense of disappointment to an overwhelming, or severe, experience of grief. Although people also refer to depression as existing along a continuum from mild to severe, sadness and depression are not the same thing. In order to more fully appreciate the value of sadness as a messenger, it is important to understand how it differs from depression. Depression is a clinical diagnosis made on the basis of reported and observed behaviors and internal experiences. It is the most commonly diagnosed emotional disorder and is estimated to affect 10 percent of the population. Specific symptoms associated with depression may include:

- Persistent anxiety, sadness, or a sense of emptiness
- Feelings of hopelessness, pessimism, worthlessness, guilt, and/or helplessness
- Loss of interest in previously enjoyed activities
- Problems with sleeping or eating
- Impaired concentration, memory, or decision making
- Decreased energy
- Irritability or restlessness
- Thoughts of death and/or suicidal thoughts or intentions

While depression may be stimulated by a perceived loss, the symptoms generally persist long after the identified stress has passed. A diagnosis of clinical depression is made when symptoms are present for more than two weeks, and when the emotional state represents a clear difference from a previous level of functioning. It is also acknowledged that in some situations involving major loss, such as the death of a loved one, the grief associated with the loss, rather than a true clinical depression per se, may account for the symptoms.

Depression is a painful condition for many people: up to 15 percent of those diagnosed with depression make a serious suicide attempt. While they may not be fully understood, the chemical changes experienced by individuals who suffer from clinical depression appear to be quite profound and require intervention. Left untreated, depression may improve over time, but often it does not. The hopeful news is that with proper treatment—often involving a combination of medication and psychotherapy—depression can be transformed and most individuals can be restored to normal, productive functioning.

Many resources are available on the subject of clinical depression, and interested readers are encouraged to explore further. Perhaps the most important thing to remember in differentiating depression from sadness is that clinical depression is, by definition, an illness. Medical and psychological models view depression as a major problem and seek to eliminate it to restore functioning and peace to patients suffering from the disorder. Sadness is neither a disorder nor an illness, but its association with depression sometimes makes it hard for people to regard it as the healthy, normal messenger it is.

Sadness is a normal human response to the experience of loss. In its role as messenger, sadness informs us that we are experiencing the loss of something we regard as having value, and it invites us to pay attention to this truth. Although sadness is not depression, despair, grief, or despondence, these reactions sometimes follow the message delivered by sadness.

To further complicate the distinction between sadness and depression, many individuals who are suffering from clinical depression are also experiencing sadness in response to some personal loss or losses. In such cases, relieving the symptoms of depression is often an important first step to being able to allow sadness to guide the person to a more peaceful place.

SAD, NOT BAD: LEARNING ABOUT SADNESS

The experience of loss is common to all people. Some losses are passive events in that they occur without any action on our part. Even if we stand still and do nothing, we will eventually experience some loss: seasons change, friends move away, relatives get old and frail. Eventually, death will come to someone we cherish. Other losses are a by-product of circumstances that force us to move on, leaving behind things we value. Events that bring us happiness come to an end: we graduate from school, end a season at a summer camp, finish a good book.

Still other losses are related to active choices we make in our own best interest. We may go away to college, distancing us from family; move to a new home, leaving neighbors behind; or take a better job, bringing an end to workplace friendships. Sadness is a part of each of these experiences, and when it is attended to, sadness can guide us to make satisfying choices to address the experience of loss.

These ordinary changes, which stimulate the sense of loss, often lead to fulfilling responses. When a favorite season passes, holidays and rituals of the new season help us celebrate the change. When we are separated from friends and loved ones, spontaneous calls, emails, and letters help us keep in touch. When someone dies, a funeral, memorial service, and personal sharing among the living help us celebrate the sad event. Using the word *celebrate* to describe a response to sadness may seem odd, but only if we regard a celebration as a necessarily upbeat and joyous affair. Any time we give special attention and consideration to an event, it represents a celebration of its importance. These few examples illustrate how the sadness arising from commonplace losses is often experienced—and listened and responded to—organically, without much conscious thought. It is the natural state of all messengers to coexist with experience and action in a fluid union.

While the experiences mentioned above are commonplace, they are not really everyday experiences. Sadness also speaks to us when we encounter much more subtle and much more frequent losses. Whenever we are faced with a choice to do one thing that prevents us from doing something else we enjoy, sadness is present. Simple examples might include having to miss a social event or a concert because of a previous commitment, or missing a workout at the gym because of an unavoidable meeting. Sometimes we have to choose between two enjoyable options, such as when one child's soccer game conflicts with another child's track meet, or when a favorite band is playing on the same night as a friend's wedding.

I experienced this type of sadness not too long ago, when a friend of mine called me three hours before game time to offer me seats right behind home plate for a Nationals baseball game.

My prior plans to get together with friends meant I had to decline the offer. Perhaps there was some anger in having to turn down the tickets—the conflict did feel somehow unfair—but I was also sad about missing the opportunity to see the game from the best seats in the house. Whenever we speak of "missing" something or someone, we are referring to a loss, and sadness is not far away.

As with each of the other messengers, our early learning and prior experience greatly influence our ability to listen to sadness. Sadness is a natural and frequent visitor in the lives of most children. When a playdate comes to an end or when toys must be put away or when a stick is taken away for safety's sake, most children feel sad. Crying is not an uncommon response, though these situations are often confusing because the child may also be feeling angry about the perceived injustice of it all. Regarding the sadness, many parents and caregivers have found strategies for easing the separation from the friend, toy, or stick. Some children benefit from advance notice about saying good-bye or putting the toys away. Safety issues can sometimes be explained in language the child can understand.

Empowering children to take an active role in the separation process often helps them find their own responses to sadness. Children may hug the friend or put the toys away for safekeeping. They may bargain with the adults for more time or broker a deal to get together again. Or the child may pitch a fit and create a loud, unpleasant scene as he or she is removed from the situation. After the tantrum subsides, parents and caregivers are presented with an opportunity to teach the child about the emotions involved and the behaviors that follow. In some fashion, the child can be taught that it is natural to feel sad, but there are more useful ways to express the feeling. The child can learn that a tirade will not stop the loss and that momentary sadness can actually help the child prepare for separations, endings, and good-byes.

Sometimes parents make the mistake of overindulging a child's desire to avoid the losses he or she faces. They may give in to the child's demands for more time with a friend, or allow a child to continue playing with a toy or game when it inconveniences others. These approaches to endings, separations, and good-byes give children an unfair and unrealistic notion about their power to control the small, sad changes that are part of everyday life. In the interest of pleasing or appeasing the child, these parents miss the opportunity to help the child develop an appreciation of the common experience of sadness, and they delay the challenge of learning how to respond to the messenger in a healthy manner.

Another parenting pitfall where sadness is concerned is the tendency to try to shield children from the reality of sadness. This usually occurs with such universally sad events as a divorce or the death of a relative. Often parents will rush to reassure a child that things will be OK without directly attending to the feelings involved, which typically include sadness. Without giving their children the opportunity to talk about their feelings, parents may tell sons and daughters that their lives will be essentially unchanged after the divorce or that their deceased grandparent is in heaven.

Given the chance to express difficult, painful feelings in a safe and supportive setting, children will invariably find an acceptable, generally peaceful balance. When they are not given this opportunity, children come to believe that their feelings are not valued, and if they are not valued, they must not be very valuable. When the sadness around sad events is not expressed and validated, the feeling is buried or misdirected, and its potential value as a messenger and guide is hidden away.

A number of years ago I worked with a couple who were concerned about their adolescent daughter's sudden emotional changes. She was fourteen years old and had just started high school when her formerly cheery and carefree mood turned sullen and withdrawn. In the course of providing background information, the couple mentioned that their daughter had a mild neurological disorder that caused her to walk with a slight limp, though she had participated in most childhood sports and activities without any accommodations. When I asked how the teenager felt about her condition, the parents sheepishly admitted they had never discussed it with her.

These were loving, devoted parents, yet they had never talked to their child about the physical condition that made her stand out from her peers. When asked why they had never discussed it with her, the parents said they didn't want to make her feel sad or bad about herself. When they finally addressed the issue with the girl, they learned that her feelings about the limp were the source of her recent mood changes. Because her parents had never talked about her limp with her, she had assumed the topic was off-limits at home, and she kept her feelings about it to herself. With some guidance, the girl was able to talk about how her limp made her feel self-conscious in school, and she was able to express her sadness about being different from other students. When the feelings were out in the open, the girl and her parents expressed a sense of relief and were free to explore her concerns openly and without shame.

Some parents actually try to evoke a feeling of sadness in a child as a form of controlling the child's behavior. This parental strategy is commonly known as guilt-tripping, and it is an indirect and dishonest way of trying to get someone to do something when that person really doesn't feel like it. When parents take this approach, they are essentially telling their children they should feel sad about not doing something or not taking some action, such as doing a chore or sending a thank-you note to a relative. In truth, the child really doesn't feel particularly sad about the behavior, so the guilt-trip is an attempt to make the child feel bad about not feeling sad! Pretty confusing stuff, this, which only clouds the relationship with sadness. In the interest of helping the child develop a healthy relationship with his or her feelings, it would be better to set clear expectations and clear consequences for child. If it is important to the parents for the child to send a birthday card to Aunt Nelly, then making TV watching contin-

gent on completion of that task will get the job done more efficiently than the emotional manipulation of a guilt-trip.

Perhaps the harshest parental response to sadness comes from
parents who see the emotion only as a "waste of time." Typically,
because of their own early experiences, these parents have little
tolerance for a child's sadness and do not allow any expression of
this natural response to loss. The cliché "I'll give you something
to cry about!" is all too real in the lives of children whose parents have no regard for the importance of helping a child learn
how to respond to sadness in a meaningful way. They minimize
the immediacy of a child's experience of the world and fail to see
how the sadness of something as simple as a lost toy is quite real
to the child. If expression of sadness is followed by a parental response that induces fear, a child very quickly learns to deny or to
hide this normal emotion. Since it leads to parental disapproval
or worse, sadness is viewed as an unsafe feeling, and it becomes a
messenger to be avoided rather than listened to.

THE COURSE OF SADNESS

In its role as a member of the vigilant triad, sadness attempts
to guard against the human tendency to become overwhelmed in
a crisis of loss. When there is a perceived loss, sadness invites us
to slow down, regroup, assess the personal impact of the loss, and
make choices about going forward. In the case of a lost opportunity, such as missing the chance to go to a party, the process leading from slowing down to going forward may be relatively short
lived. When the loss involves a valued object, like a piece of jew-
elry, the process may take somewhat longer, and the sadness may
return from time to time when the loss is recalled.

In the case of the death of a loved one, it is not uncommon
for the process of stopping, regrouping, reflecting, and moving
on to last for a year or more. When someone we love dies, the
experience of the sadness may vary in intensity, becoming less
acute over time. Other aspects of life gradually come back into

focus and normal routines are resumed, but the messenger sadness usually visits us whenever there is a reminder of the loved one. One of the ways the messenger sadness shows its wisdom is in its ability to help us experience loss by guiding us to an appreciation of the people and things we hold dear.

Unfortunately, people often grow impatient with sadness and try to rush its natural progression. Even well-meaning friends and relatives may try to encourage a sad person to "get over it" or "put the past behind." This often stems from the erroneous view of sadness as the opposite of happiness rather than an emotional response to a different set of circumstances. People also have a tendency to view sadness as an inactive messenger and an emotionally frozen state. Most of us can understand and accept someone's sadness in response to a personal loss, but we tend to put a time limit on how long the sad mood should be permitted.

While each of the messengers is subject to harsh criticism on occasion, only sadness is regarded as a waste of time. The quality of slowing down associated with sadness contributes to it being viewed as an inactive emotion, though it is precisely this quality that allows sadness to deliver the messages we need to hear. We experience loss as a disruption or a break in our attachment to something or someone we value; if it had no personal value to us, the change would not be experienced as loss, and sadness would not be part of the experience. This is just another way of saying that all loss is personal in nature and disrupts our personal sense of order and familiarity. When we experience loss, we need time to assess the impact of the loss on our general sense of well-being. We also need time to consider how to best address the hurt associated with the loss, and we need time to figure out what we will do to address the empty space created by the loss.

Sadness encourages us to take the time necessary to assess, process, and address the experience of loss. Like all organic things, emotional states have a beginning, a middle, and an end. When we try to deny, avoid, or rush through the experience of sadness, we interfere with a natural and mindful response to a loss, and our actions are more likely to be reactive attempts to get away from pain rather than thoughtful efforts to decide how best to proceed. If we allow sadness to take its natural course, it will invariably lead us to the choices that make the most sense to us.

Marie

Early in my career I had a terrific job as a clinical and training staff member at Saint Elizabeths Hospital in Washington, D.C. Half of my time involved direct patient care, but the other half was devoted to teaching and supervising interns in an NIMH–funded program for training in group psychotherapy and psychodrama. Each year about ten interns were selected to participate in the yearlong intensive program, the selection process for which was highly competitive. The nature of the work with diverse and difficult patients, and the action orientation of the group therapy training, fostered close friendships and collegial relationships among the interns.

One of my supervisees was Marie, a clinical social worker by training who had come to Washington from the West Coast, where she had worked for a social service agency. She was a bright, insightful therapist and showed great creativity when directing psychodrama groups with the patients. She got along well with unit staff and was always up to date with her administrative duties. Marie was one of the shining stars of the training class and a joy to supervise.

With less than a month left before graduation, Marie started to show some uncharacteristic behavior. She seemed harried much of the time and was often late for supervision and training sessions. She didn't attend an after-work party organized by one of her fellow trainees, and she appeared to be avoiding casual conversation with the rest of the group, claiming to be swamped with paperwork on the units.

At that time I had worked at the psychodrama section for five or six years, and I had gone through several yearlong training classes and observed what happened each time the end drew near. Some of the interns would become quiet and withdrawn, while others would become overly involved in planning end-of-the-year events. Some ordinarily easygoing intern would invariably get embroiled in a fight with a staff member or another intern. Some interns would seem to vanish from view, appearing only for required sessions then retreating to the treatment wards. And other interns, like Marie, would find themselves busy to the point of being overwhelmed.

Psychotherapy supervision is not psychotherapy, but it can come pretty close at times. Becoming an effective and skilled therapist requires a healthy understanding of one's own issues and concerns. Therapists need to be aware of their own sensitivities in order to assure that they are guiding clients without letting any personal agenda or unresolved issues get in the way. It is one of the reasons why personal psychotherapy is a requirement for students in most psychology and psychiatry training programs. Unresolved issues with separations and endings can negatively affect the way a therapist handles one of the most important phases of the therapy relationship—the termination.

I shared my observations of past intern groups with Marie in one of our supervision sessions. Initially, she saw no connection to her own behavior, which she regarded as an effort to tie up loose ends with her patients and their treatment teams.

"What about the loose ends with your friends in the program?" I asked.

She minimized the issue but agreed to tell me about her general experience with good-byes throughout her life. Marie's father was a career military officer, and her family had moved every couple of years throughout her childhood and adolescence. She had attended about a dozen different schools and had said good-bye to friends more often than most people do in a lifetime. Typically, her father would get his reassignment and the family would pack and move within a couple of weeks, sometimes in the middle of the school year. For Marie, friendships were fleeting interactions to be enjoyed briefly and forgotten about once they were gone.

When I asked Marie how she had felt about the many changes and the frequent loss of friendships she had experienced, she replied: "What difference does it make how I felt? I couldn't do anything about it."

With little prompting Marie saw where I was going. Throughout her childhood no attention had been paid to the many good-byes she experienced. Perhaps it was related to a family strategy borne of her father's choice of a career. Frequent endings were just a part of their life, and ignoring the sadness associated with moving away from friends may have felt like the most efficient way to avoid pain. Whatever the reason for the strategy, it ultimately didn't work for Marie.

Sitting in the supervision room she acknowledged through her tears that saying good-bye to new friends was always sad, always difficult, and always something she suffered silently. She said that she would try not to get attached to people, but her natural curiosity and friendly spirit made her efforts to keep her emotional distance futile. When it came time to say her good-byes there were boxes to pack and arrangements to be made. Farewells with friends became a fleeting, superficial affair, with no opportunity to acknowledge or attend to the sadness associated with the losses.

The discussion eventually led to her sadness about the conclusion of the training year and the endings she would be facing in just a few weeks. Marie had already acknowledged that efforts to avoid the sadness of good-byes in the past didn't make the losses any less painful; avoidance only drove the feelings inside and out of view and made the experience of the sadness a completely private affair. Without prescribing any specific course of action, I invited Marie to consider other ways to express her sadness and suggested that the end of the training year offered her a number of opportunities to do just that.

She listened, first to me, then to her own feelings as she let the messenger sadness guide her actions. She made time to connect with her fellow interns and with the training staff, sharing her feelings about what the relationships had meant to her. When it came time for her to say good-bye to me, Marie gave me a beautiful candleholder, which she felt represented our training relationship.

There is no meter for objectively measuring emotional pain, but it is probably the case that Marie's sadness was no less painful for having been expressed more directly than she had in the past. Saying good-bye and the loss associated with it always hurts, but by listening to the messenger, Marie found she could exercise her choice to express the sadness in a more satisfying way, and she could say good-bye in a manner that honored the wonderful relationships she had made over the previous year.

There is a tragic footnote to this story. A couple of years after her graduation from the program, Marie died in a traffic accident. I was very upset by the news of her death, and after sitting with the messenger sadness for a time, I found expression for my feelings in several ways. I spent time alone with my feelings, and I shared thoughts and feelings with colleagues and friends who had known her and were also mourning the loss. I wrote an obituary for the psychodrama association newsletter, giving other members of the community a glimpse of Marie's spirit to the best of my ability. I burned a candle in her honor in the candleholder she had given me. Sadness stayed for a while, gradually running its course. But even today, when something reminds me of Marie, I try to be mindful of the messenger sadness and sit with the memory of her. From time to time, the sadness encourages me to share some of my memories with people who never had the chance to meet Marie, as I have in this chapter.

QUIET VIGILANCE

In its effort to inform and guide us, the messenger sadness takes a different approach from the other members of the vigilant triad, anger and fear. Since they are closely related to the flight-fight mechanism of the brain, anger and fear sometimes encourage a relatively swift response to the perceived injustice or threat. Indeed, some unfair and threatening situations require quick action as a matter of survival. This is not the case with sadness.

When there is loss, especially in the case of sudden loss, there is often an immediate response, which may include an intense need for action sometimes bordering on panic or frantic activity. These actions are normally a response to the sense of being out of control and are more typically reactions to anger or fear than to sadness. When the usefulness of these actions runs its course, sadness remains attentive to the loss, encouraging us not to act, but to *stop* acting. Another way of considering the difference between sadness and the other members of the triad is to view anger and fear as a response to *the presence* of something, whereas sadness is a response to *the absence* of something.

Whenever there is a loss, a void is created by the absence of the valued person or thing. The void can be attended to only by spending time with it, and sadness encourages us to do so. For people who are used to responding actively to a challenge or crisis, sitting still without an active response may be experienced as being out of control. The sense of being unable to control or influence a situation can be extremely painful, but this is precisely the point of the message that sadness delivers. Ultimately, we do not have the power or the ability to control our sadness in response to loss. The best we can do is experience it and make choices about how to go on.

Sadness informs us that something of value is gone and invites reflection upon the loss. By encouraging a "time out" from the ordinary pace of daily life, sadness allows us to consider what it is that makes the loss painful. It raises the question: What were the qualities of the departed person or the object that gave them their value and made them precious to us? This can be a complex and difficult question for it draws into focus the fact that we often take for granted the very things we cherish, and we appreciate them only when they are no longer available to us. As Joni Mitchell put it, "You don't know what you got 'til it's gone."

No particular "homework" is required to find an opportunity to learn from the wisdom of the messenger sadness. Loss is never far away, and a willingness to listen is all that is required. One cannot get past the first page of any newspaper without reading of some loss. War, famine, natural disasters, crime, and business crises are the daily themes of front-page stories. While the newspaper reader may have no personal connection to the people whose lives are affected by such losses, a brief moment of reflection can usually evoke some sadness for the plight of the victims. If a news story feels too remote to warrant a visit from the messenger, a person can simply wait a short while before loss appears in his or her personal life. Missed opportunities, disappointments, financial concerns, lost objects, and the small failures of everyday life provide ample opportunity for personal encounters with sadness and give each of us the chance to learn from the visitor.

In time, the pain of loss yields to the wisdom that sadness has to offer. Sadness encourages us to reflect upon the loss and guides us toward choices for the future. It invites us to spend time with the question posed earlier in this section: What were the qualities of the lost person or object that gave it value and made it precious to us? In the process of trying to answer this question, a second question comes into focus: What choices can be made in response to the loss? In the case of a one-of-a-kind ring that is now gone, perhaps it was the rarity or the beauty that made it special. If the loss cannot be directly replaced, what can be done to restore or replace the sense of beauty and specialness that were embodied in the ring?

Where the loss involves another person, gone through distance, circumstance, or death, the process of reflection may focus on the qualities of the departed person that made him or her special, unique, or otherwise beloved by us. No person can be replaced in whole, but sadness asks us to consider making choices to bring people with similar qualities closer in our lives, or to consider the qualities we loved about the lost person and strive to embody those qualities in ourselves.

Sadness is a powerful messenger; in times of profound loss the pain it evokes may feel like an excruciating emotional state that will never end. But given the opportunity to do so, sadness can eventually guide us beyond the immediacy of the loss and can help us make important choices that honor the people and things no longer with us. By inviting reflection on the true value of that which is lost to us, sadness can encourage us to consider the precious and tenuous nature of the things we hold dear and can highlight the importance of making choices that enrich our lives.

FEAR

THE MESSENGER OF THE UNKNOWN

Fear is something to be moved through, not something to be turned from.
—Peter McWilliams

In 1933, Franklin Delano Roosevelt told a weary nation, "We have nothing to fear but fear itself." The president's bold statement was inspirational and uplifting, offering the hope of a brighter future for America. It was also an outrageous lie. At the time of his speech, the country was in the grip of the Great Depression. Millions of Americans had plenty to fear: joblessness, homelessness, and hunger, to name just a few of the stressful uncertainties they faced. Obviously, Roosevelt's statement was meant as encouragement, urging people to remain strong and hopeful through trying times. The unfortunate victim of this statement was the messenger fear, which was once again erroneously cast as a weak and undesirable emotion.

THE PHYSIOLOGY OF FEAR

We saw in the chapter on anger how the body reacts to the perception of potential danger. When a person perceives a threat, the chemical ball starts rolling: adrenaline is released, which in turn increases the heart rate and dilates the blood vessels that lead to the large muscle groups, preparing the individual to respond to the perceived threat. When the threat is determined to be something that cannot be overpowered, the flight instinct is triggered, and the human animal does what it can to distance itself from the potential danger.

The rapid but intricate emotional response immediately preceding the flight from danger is what we refer to as fear. Fear is not weakness. It is a necessary and potentially life-preserving emotion that alerts us to the need for caution when we face an unknown situation that may be dangerous. The saying goes, "Only the strong survive." If this is so, then fear must be considered a quality of strength, for it is not only the physically toughest individuals who overcome adversity but also the individuals who have the sense to get out of harm's way.

FACING THE BOOGEYMAN:
LEARNING ABOUT FEAR

Fear is a normal human response to a circumstance that is perceived to be potentially dangerous. As an important member of the vigilant triad, fear sounds the warning alarm, encouraging caution, alertness, and an assessment of a possible threat. It is the messenger that informs us we are facing something unknown and potentially painful and invites us to respond to that reality.

Fear exists along a continuum, which ranges from mild concern to an overwhelming sense of terror. When we search for a set of misplaced keys, fear is with us. When we hear that harm has befallen a loved one, fear is with us. The experience of the fear is a matter of degree, but in all cases fear informs us that pain is a possible outcome of the present situation. Fear tells us something unknown awaits, it may be painful, and we should prepare ourselves to meet the challenge.

When a car skids unexpectedly across an icy road, anyone

driving that car would experience the sudden flash of fear. The driver's response to the crisis depends upon a number of factors, including past experiences, faith in the vehicle to provide some level of safety, and personal training in dealing with this kind of emergency. Whether the person behind the wheel is fresh out of driver's ed or is Mario Andretti, fear precedes the response. People have a strong tendency to view a feeling as being synonymous with some of the behaviors associated with it. Anger is confused with violence; love is confused with passion. Fear is immediately present in all crises, emergencies, and traumatic events; in each case, we experience a temporary sense of being out of control. Because it is associated with these unpleasant situations, fear is many times regarded as a failure to conquer a difficult situation and is therefore seen as a weakness. This is an unfortunate and very limited view of fear, since it has the potential of cutting us off from a messenger that is trying to inform and protect us.

Fear is a natural and healthy part of our childhood experiences. Nowhere is this more evident than in infancy, where the response to the experience of fear is most immediate and where the infant is presented with new and previously unknown stimuli at an amazing rate. Some of the new sensations are perceived as pleasant and experienced as happiness, but other sensations are perceived as potentially threatening and experienced as fearful. Loud noises, unpleasant smells, or new faces may be experienced as potential dangers to which the infant responds with fear, ranging from mild trepidation to the classic startle response. Crying follows, and alert caregivers respond with hugs, a soothing touch, or some other reassuring gesture. Calm is restored. In time, the child will become accustomed to the sound, smell, or visual stimulus, and fear is no longer needed to help the child find safety.

When safety and security are assured, children are free to explore, learn, and thrive. When safety is a concern, thriving takes a backseat to efforts to find comfort, reassurance, and protection. Loving parents or other caregivers welcome the job of providing safety for their children and rejoice in watching their child experience the newness of the world. But even the most attentive and caring parents cannot stop the child from facing the "boogeyman."

This boogeyman to which I refer is the personification of any fear that is ultimately unrelated to a real threat. A child's fears of the dark or of noises down the hall do not generally represent any real danger, but the child doesn't know this; to him or her, the fear is quite real. Parents respond to these fears in many different ways, but any basically healthy approach involves validating the child's fear, assuring the child of safety, and allowing the child the opportunity to find a comfortable relationship with his or her own fear, essentially making peace with the boogeyman.

Most parents are aware of the challenge of getting a child to sleep without repeated cries or demands for a visit from them. The extreme unpleasantness of this developmental stage has led some parents to climb into bed with the child, leaving only after the child has fallen asleep. Other parents have allowed the child to sleep in the parental bed for months, even years, to soothe the child's fears. Many parents have said it is simply too painful to let their children cry themselves to sleep, so they sacrifice their own comfort for what they see as a loving approach to the problem.

While these approaches may indeed be self-sacrificing and motivated by love, they are, ultimately, misguided. One of the first challenges of individuation is the problem of putting oneself to sleep. For most children this is somewhat difficult, since all of the sensations involved with lying alone in a crib in the dark are unknown and perceived as potentially threatening. If a parent has provided a clean diaper, a full belly, a soft warm bed, and a tender "Good night," however, then the child's fears are unfounded.

In order to develop the ability to listen effectively to the messages that fear has to offer, the child needs to learn the important lesson that not all fear leads to pain. In the case of putting oneself to sleep, this lesson can be learned only by discovering that nothing bad will happen as the child drifts off to sleep. Many books offer reasonable approaches to the bedtime challenge, but sooner or later it comes down to the child spending enough time alone with his or her fears to learn that the boogeyman has no real power. In so doing children learn that they can experience fear, assess the danger, and provide their own comfort.

Developing the ability to listen to fear, to accurately assess potential danger or pain, and to make effective choices to the best of our abilities may begin in early childhood, but it is a challenge that is with us our entire lives. Belief in our own ability to meet this challenge is the quality we need in order to live a life unhampered by the ordinary fears we face every day. Early learning plays an important role in the development of this belief.

One of the most difficult tasks of parenting, teaching, coaching, or mentoring is striking the balance between providing solutions to fear-inducing situations and encouraging children to find their own solutions to the challenges they face. Overprotected or overindulged children may develop unrealistic expectations of a world in which all fears are addressed by outside forces. Children who never have the opportunity to experience the empowerment that comes from finding their own solutions to situations they fear are unprepared for the uncertain circumstances they will inevitably encounter later on. Difficulties ranging from anxieties and insecurities to narcissistic expectations of being bailed out of problems are not uncommon manifestations in adult life. With appropriate guidance, most children grow to adulthood ready to take on the challenges that come their way. They are able to use judgment to assess the things they fear and creativity to find ways to deal with the unknown.

TRAUMA AND FEAR

For too many children the stability, safety, and security required to form a healthy relationship with fear are missing from their lives. For these children the everyday environment is the source of pain and danger, creating a situation in which fear is the predominant messenger. Neglect, emotional abuse, physical beatings, or sexual mistreatment create a home environment where safety can never be assumed and where constant vigilance is required. Fear must work overtime to inform the child of potential danger and prepare that child to do what he or she can to deal with what may be coming.

The creativity and courage employed by children raised in traumatic circumstances in their efforts to survive is a remarkable testament to the human spirit, but the cost is great. Experience teaches these children they cannot afford the luxury of trust and risk-taking in their efforts to connect with other people. Fear informs the young victim of abuse that people cannot be trusted, and the child remains constantly on guard against potential harm. The message that fear delivers may help the child avoid abuse in some circumstances, and it certainly helps the child address the emotional pain that accompanies misplaced trust. Avoidance, dissociation, running away, and affiliating with other wounded children are but a few of the strategies children find when they follow fear's message.

The very strategies that serve a self-protective function in childhood, however, often become an impediment to happiness later in life when the abusive caretakers are no longer an active presence. In adult life these survivors of abuse often experience a fear of being in situations that could evoke the feeling of fear. This fear of fear is usually addressed by employing any one of many strategies to keep people at a safe distance, minimizing the likelihood of interpersonal pain. Unfortunately, these distancing strategies also prevent the development of the very thing most survivors crave, namely, a safe, loving, and supportive relationship with another human being.

INTIMACY

Intimacy is practically a synonym for vulnerability. We can be loved only to the extent that another person knows us, and true interpersonal closeness requires taking the risk of allowing our most personal and private selves to be revealed. When we are open to this degree, we are also unprotected and vulnerable to tremendous pain should the other person prove unworthy of our trust. We offer our trust and take the risk because the experience of being connected to another person in a safe and loving way fulfills us.

When trust and risk are present, the messenger fear is never far away. Fear is present in every developing intimate relationship, guiding the process. It invites us to be attentive, to move at a reasoned pace, to assess the potential for pain, and to make decisions that are in our best interest. A healthy relationship with fear is not anxiety, panic, or terror; it is just the normal human response to the uncertainty of unknown territory. By listening to the messenger and following its guidance, we move into deeper levels of intimacy. People who avoid relationships altogether out of fear of being hurt can never know the joy of human intimacy. On the other hand, individuals who ignore normal fears entirely and commit to a brand-new relationship too quickly usually have unrealistic expectations of getting their needs met and often face conflict and disappointment somewhere down the road.

Whenever I work with a client whose unrealistic expectations of a new relationship seem driven by a desperate reaction to fear rather than a reasoned response to the messenger, I ask him or her if the new relationship has passed the toothpaste test. The client typically looks at me quizzically, and I respond by asking, "Does this person you can't live without squeeze the toothpaste tube from the bottom or the middle of the tube?" The client almost never knows the answer to that question, because it usually takes time for these small, ordinary, and everyday intimacies to come to light. Of course, the point I am trying to make, humorously, is that despite any initial attraction or infatuation, it takes time to really get to know about another person. Clearly, fear is not the only messenger involved in a budding relationship, but it plays an important role in helping us pace the growth of intimacy and address normal concerns as they arise.

Tim

Had his wife not insisted upon it, Tim might never have sought treatment to address the issues that were having an impact upon his marriage. After several years of being happily married, Tim's wife began to press the issue of starting a family. The couple had spoken previously about the topic in general terms, and both agreed they would have children when the time was right. Almost immediately after his wife suggested they discontinue using birth control, their previously active sex life came to a grinding halt, due entirely to Tim's avoidance. He would claim to be too busy, too tired, or too involved in something, all of which kept him away from the bedroom.

For nearly a year Tim avoided any sexual advances by his wife, and she reacted predictably. She wondered if he was having an affair, if he had lost interest in her, if he never intended to have children. Tim professed his love and devotion to her at every opportunity, reassuring her that she was the only woman in his life. After his avoidance became obvious, even to him, he shared his own confusion about his behavior. He said that he did want a family, but he expressed unrealistic concerns about timing, finances, and career issues. His wife was deeply in love with Tim, but she finally told him that she would leave the marriage if he did not make an effort to address the problem and give her a straight answer about whether she could hope to have a child with him.

Tim was one of the nicest guys you could ever hope to meet. He was handsome and personable and had a good sense of humor and a healthy range of interests. An athlete and an outdoorsman, he was both comfortable and successful in dealing with difficult and challenging situations at work and in his outdoor adventures. He was the older of two boys raised in a family that was intact until the parents divorced after the children left home. However, Tim did not feel that the divorce had had much of an impact on him. He appeared sincerely baffled about his avoidance of a sexual relationship with his wife and denied any romantic or sexual interest in anyone else.

For several weeks Tim's sessions seemed to alternate between his defending what he regarded as a normal, healthy childhood and his confusion about his apparently stalled libido. Nevertheless, I began to note an odd pattern when the discussion turned to the question of whether he wanted to start a family. Tim responded to my direct questions about this with noncommittal answers that bordered on such clichés as "Kids are what it's all about," or "I need someone to carry on the family name, right?" When I gently pressed the issue with him, noting that he hadn't really said yes or no in answer to the question, Tim's composed demeanor stepped aside and his feelings rose to the surface. Through tears, he revealed that he loved the idea of having a child, but he had serious doubts about his ability to be a good and an effective parent. He was fearful his shortcomings would damage any child he might father.

Once the discussion turned toward the issue of parenting, Tim could more fully understand his fears. He regarded his childhood as unremarkable and pleasant not because of the joyful atmosphere in his home but because of the absence of any notable conflict. His parents had been passive and, as much as possible, uninvolved in the job of parenting. They hadn't played with their sons, nor had they taken an interest in their activities. They had never organized family outings or vacations and both had been consumed with their jobs. Tim could not remember a single discussion with either of his parents regarding emotions or normal childhood anxieties.

Tim did well in school and was active in sports, which provided some social outlet, though he could not recall his parents attending a single sporting event. His brother was not as gifted as Tim was; he was more sullen, withdrawn, and aloof. Tim assumed a great deal of the parenting responsibility for his little brother, helping him with schoolwork, protecting him from bullying, and trying to guide him, even long after the brother became an adult. Nonetheless, his brother had made different choices and struggled with substance abuse, relationship problems, and compulsive gambling up to the time of our sessions.

Once the door was opened, Tim spoke freely about the emotional desert in his home, admitting he had always assumed that his parents stayed together for the children's sake. In relatively short order, it became clear that fear was speaking to Tim, but he was having difficulty knowing how to react to the messenger in any manner other than the classic avoidance response. The sexual issues in his marriage had nothing to do with sex per se.

Tim had no real models for effective parenting, and he regarded his one effort at assuming the parent role with his brother as a colossal failure. Tim believed he had somehow inherited the "ineffective parent" gene, and he couldn't bear the idea of raising a child who might suffer because of his own inadequacies.

It would have been useless and inappropriate to try to reassure Tim that he had the "stuff" necessary to be a good parent. He never would have believed it, and how could I possibly know if it were true? Instead, we focused on helping him develop a better relationship with fear, an emotion he regarded as a weakness to be avoided. Once he started listening to his fear, he was able to see that it made perfect sense for him to doubt his own parenting abilities, based on poor models and his experience in a parenting role he should never have had to assume. As he listened further, he began to see that fear was a feeling and a messenger, not a jail sentence. Good parenting was an unknown experience, and he was right to be cautious about moving into the role. He began to consider that there were things he could do to learn more about what parenting involved in order to make a more informed choice about whether it was something he wanted for himself.

Tim's wife's sister had a young child, and Tim used the opportunity to log some "rug time" with his nephew. The therapeutic assignment we came up with was simple: get on the rug and play with the child—Legos, coloring, whatever the little boy wanted to do. Fear had spoken to Tim, he listened to the concerns it raised, and he responded to it by finding a safe setting in which to try out one of the essential requirements of parenting, namely, being able to play with a child.

Had the experience been unpleasant, Tim might have had to try a few more activities before acknowledging that parenting was simply something he was not interested in. Tim loved the playtime with his nephew, however, and it inspired him to learn more about what was required for effective parenting. He read a couple of books, went online to consult parenting resources, talked to young parents, and spent more time with his nephew. Eventually, Tim came to realize what all good parents know: fear is a healthy part of parenting. Not only is it OK to be afraid at times, it is *important* to be afraid. A good relationship with fear helps parents find creative and effective solutions to the many uncertainties involved in raising a child.

When Tim ended treatment with me he had resumed a sexual relationship with his wife and had come to understand that he had many other options for addressing his fears associated with potential parenting. Some time later I received a birth announcement from Tim and his wife, proud parents of a baby girl. This happy ending may seem a bit sappy, but it would have been just as fulfilling if, listening to his fear, Tim realized he simply did not want to have a child and he would have to face the tough consequences that his decision held for him. Listening to fear never guarantees a particular outcome; it only helps us assess a situation honestly and gives us the opportunity to choose from the options available to us.

SEEKING OUT FEAR

If the reader is still not convinced that fear is anything other than a human weakness, then how does one explain why so many people intentionally seek out and welcome fear-inducing experiences? Many of the activities people engage in for entertainment or recreation are intimately involved with the experience of fear. Anyone who has ever enjoyed a roller coaster ride knows that fear is part of the fun. Other examples include such thrill-seeking sports as rock climbing, skydiving, or big wave surfing.

People who engage in adventure sports often speak of the "rush" involved in some aspect of their chosen activity, like shooting a rapid in kayaking or hitting maximum velocity in skydiving. Individuals who enjoy this rush sensation are intentionally creating the release of adrenaline in their bodies by engaging in fear-inducing activities in which the risk is controlled to a greater or lesser degree. The fact that the biochemical event is experienced as thrilling or enjoyable is a matter of the way the individual frames the activity. It is obvious that one person's thrilling bungee jump is another person's idea of a terrifying nightmare.

While these extreme sports are dramatic examples of seeking out fear, most people can point to everyday activities in which they have processed and experienced fear as either a benign or an enjoyable emotion. Fear is present whenever a responsible driver is behind the wheel of a car, though it does not ordinarily detract from the driving experience. Activities like public speaking, dealing with superiors at work, or trying a new recipe typically involve the messenger fear, although they are not necessarily experienced as unpleasant or a reason to flee. In fact, when these ordinary experiences of dealing with unknown outcomes turn out well, they can be quite empowering and can encourage us to see what else we are capable of.

Learning to regard fear as a messenger and a guide requires spending time with it. The most difficult part of welcoming fear to our conscious, daily experience is overcoming the prejudice against fear as a weakness and therefore a "useless" emotion. Hopefully, this chapter has invited a broader view of fear and at least a beginning curiosity about its value as a messenger. In setting out to appreciate fear as a personal messenger and guide, we must always remind ourselves that fear is not something to be "conquered," but something to be listened to.

EVERYDAY FEAR

Everyone is aware of BIG fear. If we wait long enough, situations that evoke undeniable fear will probably find us. Automobile accidents, witnessing or being victimized by violence, natural catastrophes, our own serious illness or injury or a loved one's—these events trigger the biological response human beings refer to as fear. The overwhelming biological experience is temporary and is eventually followed by responses ranging from frozen compliance to some form of action. Everyone is aware of this kind of fear, and unfortunately, many people regard it as fear's only form.

If we want to learn about fear as a messenger and guide, however, we must become aware of fear in its more routine appearance, at other points on the spectrum of intensity. We must remind ourselves that fear is a normal response to the unknown and the uncertain outcome it portends. Once we accept this notion, we simply need to pay attention to circumstances in which we experience an inability to exercise control over the outcome to a greater or lesser degree.

The first day at a new job is an example most people can relate to. The excitement of meeting new people, learning new skills, furthering one's career, or just making money is usually joyful and regarded as a positive experience. Remember, though, that fear is a part of this positive experience as well, for where there is uncertainty, there is fear. Most people would ask themselves: "Will the new people accept me? Will the job be challenging enough or too challenging?" These normal concerns are part of the experience, and the questions can never be answered for certain until we know the lay of the land. There is no particular value in focusing solely on these uncertainties, but there is similarly no value in ignoring them altogether.

Attending to the questions can allow us to take stock of and be honest with ourselves as we approach a new opportunity. One person might decide to proceed slowly, gradually assessing the politics and social network at the new job before revealing much about his or her personality. Another person might approach the job with little inhibition and little concern for the social or political milieu. As a messenger, fear does not offer cookie-cutter responses to all unknown situations. Rather, it invites personal reflection and encourages people to make the choices that make the most sense to them, even if the choice is simply to "wait and see."

Perhaps the easiest way to begin a dialog with everyday fear is to look for the "white lie." Virtually everyone distorts the truth on occasion, often with benign or compassionate intent. Distortion or omission of facts in the form of exaggeration or minimization is a common experience. Some people are unaware they are doing this, while others are aware of the small deceptions. Almost all people, however, pay little attention to the messenger fear that stimulates the lie.

Before I start sounding like some "holier than thou" preacher, let me say that I have no doubt there are many situations in which minor distortions of the truth may be the most compassionate or thoughtful thing to do. All I am really saying here is that the white lie presents an opportunity for any of us to appreciate the role of fear as a messenger. Make a mental note the next time you catch yourself altering the absolute facts in your discussion with another person. Later, when you have time to reflect on the white lie, ask yourself what fear was trying to tell you.

- What uncertain outcome were you trying to address by intentionally leaving out facts or giving a false impression?
- Were you concerned about hurting the other person or about what that person might have thought of you or someone else?
- What might have happened if you had told the bare truth?
- Would you have presented the facts in the same way if you had considered these things earlier?

I offer this simple exercise to illustrate how commonplace the messenger fear is, and how listening to what it has to say can make us more mindful of our choices and our actions. If we understand and are comfortable with fear as the messenger of the unknown in our everyday lives, we may have a better appreciation of fear's value and importance when we are faced with more challenging uncertainties.

DIVERGENT REACTIONS TO A UNIVERSAL FEELING

On the morning of September 11, 2001, virtually every single American was visited by the messenger fear. The terrorist threat to the country was sudden and unexpected, and the immediate consequences were unknown and potentially even more devastating than the horrible attacks on the World Trade Center and the Pentagon. In the Washington, D.C., suburb where I reside, individual responses within hours of the crisis were varied. Some people left town as soon as possible, fearing more attacks. Many parents rushed to take their children home from school. Other people stayed glued to their radios and TVs, anxiously awaiting further details that indicated the government had assumed some sense of control over the crisis. No one response could be called universally right or wrong; each person responded to his or her own fear in a personal way.

The most dramatic examples of different responses to the immediate crisis were seen at the sites of the tragedy. Since many of the employees at the Pentagon are active-duty or former trained military personnel, a number of the victims of the attack quickly organized themselves to attempt to rescue trapped coworkers and to facilitate an orderly and rapid evacuation. Some of their colleagues, however, responded with understandable panic. At the World Trade Center, survivors fled the scene of the attack as quickly as possible, following their natural instinct to distance themselves from the still dangerous burning towers. Yet many trained firefighters and police officers rushed into the same burning buildings in an effort to save lives, putting their own lives in mortal danger.

Every person affected by the terrorist attacks was visited by the messenger fear, and each followed his or her own course of action. The firefighters, police, and other crisis-response professionals experienced fear like everyone else, but they had spent many hours training themselves to respond differently from most other citizens. Their heroic acts were the tangible manifestations of their choice to respond to the messenger fear with decisive action, even though many paid the ultimate price for that courageous choice.

Training and preparation can influence our responses to the messenger fear. This is true in any occupation or activity, from parenting to firefighting. Ultimately, the messenger fear provides us with the same opportunity each of the five messengers offers: the opportunity to choose. Where fear is concerned, the choice involves how we will approach situations with unknown and potentially painful consequences. Fear does not instruct everyone to respond to the same potential threat in the exact same way. It is a personal messenger, with a private relationship with each human being, and it offers each of us the opportunity to choose from the options available to us.

Some unknown circumstances hold the potential for excitement and adventure. Other unknown scenarios offer only unpleasant or hurtful outcomes. Still other unknown situations can lead to true intimacy with another person. Fear offers guidance in all of these challenging life events. A healthy understanding of fear and a clear and welcoming relationship with the messenger can help us assess our options honestly and respond to the unknown in the manner that makes the most sense to us.

THE DESIRED DUO

Reason has not tamed desire: It is as strong as ever.
—Arthur Keith

*G*iven the opportunity to choose from a menu of emotions, most people would choose happiness or love over anger, sadness, or fear. This is related to the fact that happiness and love are often erroneously seen as goals or objectives rather than a normal human response to certain life circumstances. They are no better or no worse than any of the other messengers, but the life events that evoke happiness and love are usually experienced as more enjoyable and are thus more desirable, which is why I present them as the "Desired Duo" of emotions.

It is easy to see how happiness and love have come to be regarded as good feelings, though the notion of "good" vs. "bad" feelings is as false when applied to the desired duo as it is when applied to the vigilant triad. Conceptualizing the desired duo as good feelings and the vigilant triad as bad feelings sets up a self-defeating

63

dynamic in which some of our feelings are allowable and others are prone to rejection and harsh judgment. As was shown in the previous three chapters, the messengers of the vigilant triad are valuable and important, and their wisdom and guidance is always in our best interest. This is also true of the desired duo, and while happiness and love should not be thought of as good feelings, their messages often have a great deal to do with feeling good.

Anger, sadness, and fear are primarily concerned with safety and security, whereas happiness and love are chiefly concerned with informing us about experiences and actions that require, to a greater or lesser degree; curiosity, risk-taking, and trust. Unfortunately, this is not what many people want to hear about the desired duo. Some people regard happiness as a right, and they feel they are being cheated if happiness is not readily available or easily attained. Love is often seen as a valuable prize that can be achieved or won through charm, manipulation, or conquest. Happiness and love may feel good, but they are neither rights nor goals, and each of them requires our active involvement in ways that are at times uncertain and challenging.

Happiness and love are often thought of as easy or carefree emotions, but the conditions that allow for their appearance require an element of risk. Early life

lessons and experiences play a critical role in creating
the internal environment necessary for the desired duo
to make their presence known. For many people, issues
related to trust, safety, and security must be addressed
before a healthy relationship with the desired duo can
be established.

As messengers, happiness and love appear in response to experiences of well-being and selflessness.
They often stimulate an appetite for more experiences
that will assure their return appearances. Although
many times the messengers of the vigilant triad take
precedence, the guidance of the desired duo can inform
the choices we make to allow happiness and love to be
frequent visitors in our lives.

When they exist in harmony with the vigilant triad,
the messengers of the desired duo play important roles
in helping us achieve balance in our lives, and they
are of critical importance in the formation of healthy
relationships. In order to fully appreciate what happiness and love have to offer, we must take them down
from the pedestal we often place them on and see them
as they truly are. The next two chapters—"Happiness:
The Messenger of Well-Being" and "Love: The Messenger of Selflessness"—offer an opportunity to reflect
upon the nature and wisdom of the desired duo.

HAPPINESS

THE MESSENGER OF WELL-BEING

The foolish man seeks happiness in the distance, the wise grows it under his feet.

—James Oppenheim

In the family of messengers, happiness holds both a unique and a dubious status. It is the one emotional state that is often viewed as a goal in and of itself. No one strives for anger, sadness, fear, or even love, but the pursuit of happiness is considered not only a noble quest but also an inalienable right! Any goal, by definition, exists somewhere beyond the present, outside of one's immediate grasp. When happiness is viewed in this all too familiar light, it keeps the emotion at arm's length and prevents the messenger from offering the wisdom and guidance that come to us, not from some outside source, but from within ourselves.

THE CHEMISTRY OF HAPPINESS

The subjective experience of happiness is present in varied physical states. One person might find happiness in a rugged physical event, such as mountain climbing, while another person's happiness may present itself in a passive activity, such as reading a good book. In fact, most individuals experience happiness in a variety of different settings that range from very passive to very active pursuits. Since the subjective experience of happiness occurs in such varied settings, it is impossible to identify a particular physiological state associated with the feeling. Happiness can be found when a person's muscles are tense, breathing is rapid and shallow, and he or she is exhausted and perspiring; happiness can just as easily be found when a person's muscles are relaxed, breathing is calm and deep, and he or she is rested and refreshed.

Common to all experiences where happiness is present are a sense of enjoyment and a perception of the event as pleasant and desirable. When we are involved in an experience that is enjoyable and pleasant, our brain chemistry appears to operate in a balanced, unimpeded flow. The neurotransmitters that help send electrical signals from one nerve cell to another do their job effortlessly, and we are able to focus and apply ourselves to the experience without much difficulty. One of these neurotransmitters, serotonin, is believed to play a central role in maintaining the brain chemistry associated with engagement in activities that are experienced as enjoyable and pleasant. While some enjoyable experiences involve little physical effort and others involve great exertion, the common factor is that the experience is perceived as pleasant rather than burdensome. Happiness is the name we have given to the sense of well-being that accompanies an activity, pursuit, or condition we regard as enjoyable and desirable.

HAPPINESS VS. PLEASURE

A basic premise of this book, and a heartfelt belief of mine, is that there is no such thing as a good feeling or a bad feeling. Each of the five messengers has its own distinct role in guiding us through life's experiences, and each messenger is necessary and valuable when it appears.

Happiness is a normal human response to an experience of

well-being. As with all feelings, happiness appears along a continuum, ranging from a mild sense of contentment to the experiences referred to as joy, elation, and bliss. As a messenger, happiness informs us that the situation or circumstance we are involved in is pleasing to us, and it invites us to consider how to make satisfying choices for the future.

To truly appreciate what the messenger happiness has to offer, we must be able to differentiate it from the experience we call pleasure. This is not a simple task, since any effort to separate happiness from pleasure runs the risk of getting bogged down in an exercise of logic and semantics. Pleasure involves happiness and happiness involves pleasure, but they are not the same thing, and only one of them can truly be called a guiding messenger. See what I mean about the confusing tautology? Let me try to make the point by first discussing pleasure.

Pleasure is a response to a stimulus in the environment that evokes an enjoyable, comfortable, satisfying, or otherwise pleasurable sensation. The list of things having the power to stimulate a sense of pleasure would be voluminous, and such a list would vary with each individual. From a good haircut to a good meal to good sex, pleasure is a quickly kindled reaction or response to an external experience or event. It is easy to see how some such events are potentially life enriching. An inspiring lecture or sermon or an emotionally moving theatrical production, for example, may have the power to stimulate desirable thoughts or actions. It is just as easy to see how some pleasure-inducing events are potentially devastating: virtually each and every addictive behavior is the result of a pleasure-evoking experience taken to an unhealthy extreme.

Common to all pleasurable experiences are the following factors: the sensation is quickly accessed, the sensation is in response to some identifiable external event, and the sensation is momentary in nature. In contrast, happiness is an emotional experience that can guide us in two ways: First, it makes us aware of the people, circumstances, and things that evoke a sense of well-being; and second, it offers us an opportunity to make choices that will be fulfilling. Happiness is a response to a condition of well-being and is often experienced even when the specific stimulus or source of the happiness is not immediately present.

The momentary nature of pleasure differentiates it *from* the messenger happiness, yet in an odd paradox, momentary pleasure is also a gateway *to* happiness. Let me try, once again, to unravel this mishmash of logic and words.

Since happiness is the normal human response to a circumstance of well-being, some moments of pleasure understandably evoke the sense of comfort that can be called *momentary* happiness. In fact, there is an element of happiness in the presentation of all new pleasure. The enjoyment that comes from watching an entertaining TV show or drinking a fine wine or listening to music is momentary in nature. To the extent that such experiences evoke a sense of comfort and well-being, they can be said to involve happiness.

In the longer term, any hobby or passionate interest that contributes to someone's happiness can usually be traced to an initial pleasurable activity or event. The inspiring lecture mentioned earlier, or a single enjoyable hike in the woods, can encourage someone to pursue an interest that may become a renewable source of happiness that lasts a lifetime. In such cases, the messenger happiness invites the participant to figure out what aspect of the pleasurable moment instilled the sense of contentment and well-being. Perhaps the lecture inspired a desire to take on some satisfying pursuit, or maybe the hike in the woods stimulated an appreciation of nature. In this sense pleasure is a gateway to happiness, and listening to the messages happiness has to offer has the potential to inspire life-enhancing action.

However, the momentary nature of pleasure can also conspire to keep true happiness at bay. The immediate enjoyment experienced in a moment of pleasure sometimes exists in stark contrast to difficulties and hardships inherent in everyday life. The pursuit of pleasure-evoking experiences to avoid addressing difficulty or stress is a formula for compulsive and addictive be-havior. Alcohol, drugs, sex, work, shopping, exercise—virtually any initially pleasant experience—can become a vehicle for an unhealthy avoidance of responsibilities and relationships. When this unfortunate, yet all too frequent, pattern sets in, the indi-vidual becomes dependent upon external events or stimulation in the pursuit of pleasure. Invariably, the behavior is a source of guilt and shame and becomes a problem in and of itself. In the end, the pursuit of pleasure takes the person further and further away from the possibility of experiencing happiness.

THE FIRST UNIVERSE

The messenger happiness must be a frequent and familiar vis-itor in the lives of young children if they are to become secure and well-adjusted adolescents and adults. This is not to say that children can or should be shielded from the appearance of the more vigilant messengers, however. Besides being an impossible task, that would leave children unprepared to deal with the range of experiences they would face in later life. But as a messenger of well-being, happiness prepares children in a different way.

A child who knows happiness perceives the world as a safe and pleasant place. The late Jacob Moreno, M.D., called the child's initial experience of the world the "first universe." More-no suggested that in the earliest stages of life, children have no capacity to conceptualize the difference between themselves and the external world. It is all just one big sense-driven experience without the notion of self or other. When the child is hungry, cold, or wet, the universe is unpleasant. The child cries, the dis-comfort is addressed, and a sense of well-being is restored to the universe. In this state, happiness appears in its most primitive, essential, and unnamed form.

As the brain and body develop, children begin to experience the reality of the "second universe" and come to appreciate the existence of people and things outside of themselves. As long as happiness is a routine part of children's experiences, they will face the challenges of moving out into the world with a belief that well-being is a dependable thing, and they will feel relatively secure about exploring the world outside.

Children who know happiness from the beginning of their lives venture out with the notion that "The world is safe and usually enjoyable, my needs will be met, and when difficult things arise I can count on others to help restore a sense of safety and comfort." Such children believe in their capacity to explore, confident that their spontaneity will generally be experienced in the context of a state of well-being. Happiness is simply a natural and familiar state, and they accept that they are worthy of happiness without question.

All children experience the hardships and trials of everyday life and, like all of the feelings, happiness retreats and reappears as circumstances dictate. But children who are secure in their earliest relationship with happiness experience the messenger as an expected and welcome friend, not as a rare visitor to be regarded with caution.

LEARNING ABOUT HAPPINESS

Unfortunately, the secure relationship with happiness described above is not the reality that many children experience. As with all of the five messengers, the early environment plays a big part in teaching children about happiness and in establishing conceptions and expectations that can have a long-lasting impact. In the chapter on fear, I discussed how a sense of safety and security is a prerequisite for a child's freedom to explore and learn. Safety and security are also required if happiness is to make its appearance.

In the card game of life, the need for survival trumps the desire to thrive. In environments where aggression, violence, or abuse are a routine and anticipated part of life, fear is a necessary and frequent messenger that urges caution, avoidance, or other strategies in an individual's effort to remain safe. In such an unstable and potentially dangerous situation, a sense of well-being is all too infrequent, and happiness is all too rare.

Children raised in such settings are not familiar enough with the pleasant, comfortable, and satisfying experiences known in healthy families; therefore, they know little about ordinary happiness. Without the guidance of happiness, these children are typically emotionally guarded and have difficulty forming relationships based on trust and mutual well-being. In adolescent and adult life, children raised in fear-inducing families remain unable to benefit from the guidance of happiness. Some individuals come to rely upon various self-protective strategies designed to avoid pain and to respond to the need for self-protection; such reliance effectively keeps the possibilities for happiness at bay. Social isolation, a veneer of toughness, a hostile attitude, or extreme compliance—all are among the many strategies that serve this purpose.

Other individuals become more frantic and desperate in their efforts at self-care. Unfamiliar with the messenger, they mistake pleasure for happiness and are prone toward risky, thrill-seeking, and dangerous activities. Many individuals in recovery from drug, alcohol, or sex addiction report a sense of feeling fearful in their families during childhood. Notably, most addicts in recovery likewise eventually acknowledge that they know very little about how to have a good time without the addictive behavior.

It is not only abusive and hostile early environments that affect a child's growing connection with happiness. Other early settings, while not as overtly threatening, can have a strong influence on this important budding relationship with the messenger. Some parents or caregivers are sadly limited in their ability to provide an environment in which happiness can be a frequent visitor. Social, physical, and environmental stress can create overwhelming obstacles that some parents cannot find a way out of. Poverty, for example, creates financial stress, which may contribute to a constant sense of anxiety or despair. In an environment where fear and sadness are a routine part of daily life, happiness is not free to flourish and may make only fleeting visits.

Events and circumstances that create family stress and block opportunities for happiness are not limited to the poor, of course. When a major physical illness or an injury strikes a household, a similar sense of anxiety and despair may predominate the family interactions and severely limit the experience of well-being. When a parent or a caregiver suffers from an untreated severe mental illness, such as major depression or bipolar disorder, stability, safety, and security are often tenuous at best. Without these essential elements, children are not truly free to explore the environment and to discover their early capacity to experience happiness.

Some caregivers simply do not value happiness enough to encourage its presence in the lives of their children. I have worked with many clients who felt that their parents attended to the technical aspects of their needs—food, clothing, shelter, education—but never to their need for emotional support. For some caregivers, work is the major focus of their lives, and they regard parenting as another "job." They fail to realize, however, that parenting requires more than attention to the technical aspects of the "job," and they wrongly assume it can be best approached with limited attention to emotions. Others feel trapped by their parenting responsibilities: they feel obligated to provide for their child's basic needs, but they resent—and therefore do not support—the carefree and lighthearted aspects of childhood.

Some parents have experienced precious little happiness in their own upbringing and tend to see little value in this important messenger. They pass this unfortunate view on to their children, who often grow into materially successful but humorless adults just like their parents. One measure of how much value a parent places on creating an environment that welcomes happiness can be seen in how often and how well they play with their children.

PLAY

The notion of play usually conjures up images of pleasant or enjoyable experiences. Whether it is a sport or a game or a musical instrument, we generally think of playing as something we do to have fun. Fun is indeed the motivation for most playful activity, but the role of play in the lives of children involves many other factors that support the often-repeated adage "Play is the job of childhood."

During my research for this section of the book I came upon a few articles that suggested play is an overvalued and overly promoted concept in early childhood education. The authors of the articles appeared to have good credentials, and the articles were presented in an academic style, with well-documented supporting literature. Essentially, the authors contend that play has not been shown to be a significant factor in the acquisition of such basic skills as knowledge of language or math. They further argue that play often involves many undesirable aspects—for example, injuries, hurt feelings, and rejection—which are not considered in romantic and idealized notions about play.

The validity of these views might make for an interesting academic debate, but where the relationship between play and happiness is concerned, they are really beside the point. In addition to the many social interactive skills children learn and practice, their imagination, spontaneity, and creativity all flourish in an atmosphere of play.

The enjoyment children experience in playful pursuits allows for a free and easy relationship with the messenger happiness. When children are having fun, particularly in an unstructured play setting, imagination and creativity are part of the process, and happiness is a major aspect of the underlying emotional experience. Imagination and creativity join forces in a process that Moreno called spontaneity, in which new, effective, and appropriate responses to a situation flow naturally. This associational bond among happiness, creativity, and spontaneity creates a self-perpetuating dynamic in which the pleasure experienced during these processes encourages more engagement in them.

Nevertheless, the critical comments of the authors mentioned above regarding the undesirable consequences of play must be considered. All play should occur within a safe and supervised context. Fairness, consideration, and similar concerns can and should be a requirement of early childhood play, and it is the responsibility of parents, teachers, and other caregivers to ensure that this is the case. While these social considerations may have little to do with happiness directly, if they are established as a condition of play settings early on, then children incorporate these principles as an expected and routine part of playful interactions in the future. When caregivers establish a healthy and supportive context for play, the happiness experienced in play includes fairness and consideration for others.

The importance of these social principles is evident throughout life, but acquiring them begins in the sandbox and the playground, where children can learn that happiness does not come at the expense of others. If this lesson is well learned in childhood, later experiences with competitive games, sports, or other life events can be rewarding without having to be mean spirited. Competitors can be free to know that the happiness experienced in the joy of winning is not derived from the loss and sadness of others.

Of course, the happiness–play connection is not limited to childhood play. Most adults allocate a portion of their time specifically to engage in playful pursuits, and for many adults these hobbies, interests, and passions offer repeated opportunities for a relationship with happiness. But even by casually observing adults at play it is easy to spot the grown-ups who have never forged a truly satisfying relationship with happiness and thus have blocked the messages that happiness tries to deliver. Consider these all too frequent examples, among others, of adult play:

• The golf partner who subtly cheats in an effort to appear more proficient than he or she truly is.

- The person who avoids any competition in which he or she is not assured of doing well.
- The poor loser who throws some adult tantrum or makes foolish excuses any time things don't go his or her way.
- The poor winner who gloats and taunts, adding insult to injury after a victory.
- The braggart who cannot stop boasting about his or her achievements.
- The exaggerator whose accomplishments are always embellished.
- The showboater whose victories are achieved with more drama than necessary.

For these adults, the vigilant triad is more actively involved in play and competition than are the opportunities for happiness.

It may sound odd to put it this way, but play is not all fun and games. Each of the five messengers can be found in some form in all types of play. Disappointment, frustration, uncertainty, limitations, and mistakes invite healthy visits from anger, sadness, and fear. All of the emotions are important, and all offer guidance, but it is the messenger happiness, stimulated by the enjoyment of the experience, which compels us to play on.

Of course, happiness is not limited to play; it is just that play is the vehicle for our earliest opportunities to learn about happiness in our interactions with others. Happiness is present wherever there is a sense of well-being and can be found in virtually all meaningful pursuits. If the lessons about happiness in interactive settings are well learned, then an element of play can be found in the most mundane and most difficult challenges.

IT TASTES LIKE MORE

Whenever something was particularly agreeable to her, my grandmother would say, in her broken English and thick Austrian accent, "It tastes like more." In her own way, Grandma Rose summed up the essential message happiness tries to convey.

When an event, situation, or circumstance is enjoyable to us and stimulates a sense of well-being, happiness appears and encourages us to attend to that reality. It invites the question, "What is it about the event that is so pleasing, and why does it create this sense of well-being?" It further asks us to consider what we might do to experience this feeling again, or to make it a more familiar and recurring presence in our lives. What can we do to satiate our appetite for more?

In most cases, the process of posing these questions and responding to their answers is organic and largely unconscious. Children who enjoy reading or math or kicking a soccer ball will develop a natural attraction to these readily available activities, and they will have ample opportunities to pursue these happiness-generating interests throughout their lifetimes. Involvement in fulfilling careers, hobbies, active parenting, and other happy long-term commitments all begin with a single moment of happiness, which leads to exploring the possibility of experiencing the happiness again and again. It is this quality of the two messengers that stimulate a desire for a recurring relationship with themselves that sets the desired duo apart from the vigilant triad. Only happiness and love taste like more.

Michael

Before he had even started college, Michael had a clear vision of what he wanted out of life, and by the time he had reached his early 30s, he had realized his vision. As he had planned, Michael attended a top university, where he majored in business, followed by an internship at a high-tech company. His next step was to secure a job with a start-up company that offered him a salary and stock options. He worked long, hard hours for several years and was in the right place at the right time when his company hit it big, riding the dot-com wave at the end of the millennium. When a large, established tech firm eventually purchased his company, Michael and his associates became financially secure for the rest of their lives. He bought a Porsche Boxter and a vacation home at the beach and married the woman he had been dating for a few months. When he came to see me, Michael was working part-time as a consultant to the high-tech industry. In ten short years, he had managed to get everything he had ever wanted.

Anyone would have been envious of Michael's fortunate circumstances, not to mention his car and beach house. In the evaluation interview he reported no unusual illnesses or injuries, no history of traumatic experiences, and no significant stressful events in his current life, which raised the question of why he was seeking psychotherapy. His answer to this question was simple: "I'm unhappy," he said.

Michael went on to talk about his life growing up. He was an only child who had been raised in a country-turned-suburban town on the outskirts of a major city. His parents owned a small hardware store and worked hard to provide for the family. He incorporated his parents' values and worked hard in school, as well as working weekends and summers at the store. Early on, Michael came to regard financial security as an important goal, and he set his eyes firmly on the prize. He responded to minor setbacks with renewed commitment, and Michael never lost sight of the steps necessary to achieve his desired goal. His work ethic was unimpeachable, and the rewards were abundant. But now that he had crossed the finish line, he couldn't shake the sense that something was missing.

I asked Michael about some of the things that many people consider sources of happiness. Did he have any special interests or passions? Not really. He was in good physical condition and worked out at a gym several times a week, but it was just something he did to stay in shape, not something he particularly enjoyed. When he worked for the tech company he never had any spare time for hobbies, and he had not developed any outside interests even though he now had all the time in the world.

What about friendships? Michael reported that he had "lots of friends," but his idea of friendships involved college fraternity brothers whom he rarely had contact with and business associates who lost touch with him when the business connection was no longer part of the relationship. How about people he met through his consulting work? He admitted that he had not really gotten his independent consulting work off the ground.

What about his marriage? Michael was close to tears as he admitted he was concerned about the state of his year-old marriage. He felt that he may have made a mistake when he married his wife after knowing her for only a few months, and he acknowledged they seemed to be drifting further and further apart. Why had he married her after such a short courtship? "It seemed like the thing to do, the logical next step," he replied.

And there was the crux of Michael's problem. Within a few sessions it became clear that doing what he felt needed to be done, or following the "next logical step," was a guiding principle for Michael. His parents taught and lived the value of hard work and dedication to a goal or purpose. Michael never experienced any abuse, and no one could accuse his parents of being neglectful or inattentive to his basic needs. After all, they were a constant presence in his life, either at home or at the store. Things were orderly, efficient, and secure, but little time was spent simply having fun. Happiness was not something that received any attention; people did what they did in the service of a goal, and the attainment of the goal was its own reward. Michael had never learned much about joy as an important consideration or happiness as a valuable experience.

It would be unfair to characterize Michael's childhood experiences as being totally without happiness. There was some satisfaction in a job well done and some sense of well-being in the stable and crisis-free environment in which the family lived. But there were no playful interactions to speak of, no encouragement of creativity or spontaneity, no attention paid to purely enjoyable pursuits. Hard "gainful" work was valued and praised above all other activities. Michael came to regard the feeling of happiness as a frivolous thing, not as a necessary experience and certainly not as a trusted guide.

Had Michael loved his work, his job at the tech company would have included frequent experiences of happiness. In fact, however, Michael hated the work he had been doing and had been very close to quitting when the company hit pay dirt. Regarding his marriage, Michael observed that he and his wife had retreated into more or less private worlds, and neither of them paid much attention to the relationship.

Before Michael could make choices that would lead to happiness, he needed to become more familiar with the emotion itself. I encouraged him to take advantage of his free time and simply take note of things he found enjoyable and gave him a pleasant feeling. When he expressed uncertainty about how to go about this, I suggested he follow his curiosity and explore lots of possibilities. Because Michael had neglected the notion of curiosity for curiosity's sake, it took him some time to feel comfortable with the homework. Along the way I added something he found even more difficult: I encouraged him to talk to his wife about the things she enjoyed and about things they could possibly explore together.

Michael began to notice the ordinary things he enjoyed and started to recognize happiness in everyday experiences. Something someone said or did; an interesting book or movie; some aspect of the natural environment. He and his wife started talking and addressed the growing distance between them, which led to some couples therapy work. They also found some common interests and ways of sharing time together that were pleasing for both of them.

Michael started to allow his happiness to guide his choices, which led to an interesting realization on his part: being productive was important to him and made him happy. While he knew he would never want to return to the unfulfilling work he had done previously, Michael also knew he could never be fully happy without a feeling of productivity in his life.

Michael decided to do something he had always wanted to

do, namely, become a high school teacher. Earlier he had considered the potential for happiness in being a teacher and working with teenagers, but with his eye on the goal of great financial success, he had rejected the notion of teaching as impractical. Now, however, he could allow himself to be guided by happiness, and so he pursued his dream.

The messenger might have guided another person in similar circumstances to travel around the world or to retire at a seaside villa and play golf every day, but that was not how it spoke to Michael. He took the time to learn to value happiness, and he let it direct his choices in the way that made sense to him. He ended his work with me well on his way to his second career, which was certain to be more emotionally fulfilling than the first.

I did not cite this case study to suggest that one needs to be a millionaire in order to be free to pursue his or her dreams. Michael's focus on hard work had paid off in terms of his financial security, but he had failed to realize that no one had ever promised him that all of his efforts would lead to happiness. All people have to take responsibility for meeting their own basic needs, and while money may relieve a great deal of stress, many wealthy people are also unhappy people. Happiness did not come to Michael because of his riches. It came to him because he listened for it and because he made choices that allowed for the possibility of more happiness in the future.

THE HAPPINESS SALES PITCH

As a member of the desired duo, happiness is one of the feelings that most people would like to experience as much as possible. Constant, unremitting happiness is simply not realistic, however, nor is it particularly desirable. Many life experiences require the guidance of other messengers in situations that do not invite or welcome happiness. Regarding the vigilant triad, anger helps guide us through perceived injustice, sadness helps guide us through loss, and fear helps guide us through unknown and potentially dangerous situations. When circumstances allow for it, happiness helps guide us during times of well-being and, as will be discussed in the next chapter, love helps guide us in times of selflessness.

Feelings ebb and flow, present and retreat, in response to the ever-changing and often unpredictable events that life delivers, and their guidance can help us maintain balance and peace of mind through both difficult and easy times. If we were to rely upon TV, movies, radio, print media, and popular culture for direction, however, we would probably believe that any feeling other than happiness is undesirable.

It is quite easy to see how these forms of mass communication push the notion of happiness as a goal, often trying to sell us what they would have us believe are the means to that end. The pairing of smiling, ecstatic actors with products ranging from sandwich bags to cosmetic surgery usually accompanies promises of some better quality of life. Unfortunately, the notion of happiness as something attainable through the acquisition of material things only serves to promote the notion that happiness can be purchased, possessed, or given to us by others.

I am not standing on a soapbox here to endorse antimaterialism, nor am I passing judgment on material possessions which offer comfort or entertainment. Many products and possessions give us pleasurable experiences, and many may play an important part in helping us experience or pursue happiness. What I am cautioning against, however, is the notion promoted in our culture that material possessions are a *necessary* ingredient for happiness. This can lead some people to believe their happiness *depends* upon getting things, going places, or doing something that can be objectively defined by others. Some individuals believe they are being shortchanged by not having access to this kind of happiness, which adds a sense of desperation to their quest.

The experience, wisdom, and guidance of happiness flow

in response to a sense of well-being which can be found any-where. The happiness that comes with a good conversation with a friend, for example, is as available over the kitchen table as it is on a sailboat in the Caribbean. Happiness cannot be bought or acquired or stolen, but if we are attentive to its presence at times of well-being, it can be experienced again and again.

THE POWER OF CURIOSITY

A relationship with happiness begins with awareness of the presence of the messenger. On the surface, this doesn't sound like a difficult process, but for many people, the simple question "What makes you happy?" is complicated and not easily answered. Some respond to the question in a general way, answering "my work" or "my family." Such answers may indicate the setting in which happiness is experienced, but they do not really say what it is about the work or the family that generates a sense of happiness. Other people respond by naming objects, answering "my car" or "my guitar." These answers similarly fail to identify what it is about the object that evokes happiness. Even answers such as "going bowling" or "playing poker on Friday nights" do not really specify what it is about the event that makes the participant happy.

By all means, if it is an enjoyable experience and it enriches their lives, men and women should feel free to pursue their work or strum their guitar or bowl to their heart's content. But if there is a desire to benefit from the wisdom happiness has to offer, we must try to appreciate what it is about pleasurable life experiences that we enjoy because this welcomes the presence of happiness as a messenger. As one of the desired messengers, happiness does not necessarily invite analysis. Spending a lot of time asking "Why am I happy?" may seem somewhat like dissecting a joke to see what makes it funny and losing the humor in the process. Investing time in trying to understand happiness need not be a tedious or unhappy process, though. It can be interesting and enjoyable and, more importantly, it can help us make choices that further enrich our lives.

For people whose lives have required them to be self-protective for a long time, their unfamiliarity with happiness and distrust of it will interfere with their ability to cultivate a relationship with the messenger. As stated earlier, thriving takes a backseat to surviving, and individuals who are living with the legacy of emotional mistreatment usually need help finding the sense of safety that allows for an exploration of happiness. A closer look at happiness can be undertaken only when a reasonable amount of safety is assured. At that point, the exploration begins with curiosity.

Curiosity plays a role in our relationship with happiness, and curiosity about our own experience is necessary in order for us to have a clear sense of what it is that stimulates a visit from the messenger. This is true with any experience of well-being, but by way of illustration, let's consider something as ordinary as an enjoyable walk in the park. The happiness that accompanies this pleasant event is typically experienced without much thought or self-analysis, but one could ask, "What is it about this walk in the park that brings me happiness?" Naturally, there are many possible answers to the question, and no answer is right or wrong. The only meaningful and useful answer is the one that comes to the person asking the question. She might be happy to spend time alone, free of other pressures; he might be glad simply to breathe the fresh air; she enjoys the chance to stretch her muscles; he enjoys watching birds and squirrels.

The list of answers could go on and on, but only the questioner can give the answer that has meaning to him- or herself. The answer to the question, whatever it may be, offers important information and potential guidance for someone who wants more experiences with happiness. It invites more curiosity and follow-up questions: "What can I do to have more time with myself, breathe more fresh air, watch more squirrels? How can I make choices that will allow me to experience this again? How can I have this experience even if a walk in the park is not an option?"

Asking the first question does not automatically lead to an easy answer. Other commitments, time demands, or obligations may make it difficult for someone to allocate personal resources to the pursuit of even relatively ordinary opportunities for happiness. These other responsibilities may even be sources of happiness in and of themselves. Each person must find the balance that allows for experiences of happiness in a way that is personally fulfilling and satisfying. Curiosity and self-inquiry simply remind us of the things we should consider in striking such a balance, since complete denial of happiness is usually a route to frustration and resentment.

Some people have enough time to pursue opportunities for happiness but are uncertain about how to go about doing so. Individuals who have come through difficult times, recovered from hardships endured in childhood, embraced sobriety after years of addiction, or have simply never learned to value happiness often face considerable difficulty in knowing what to do to be happy, even when they feel ready to try. For these individuals, curiosity is usually an essential element in their new learning. They often need encouragement to allow their natural curiosity to explore interests, activities, events, or relationships that might lead to the experience of happiness.

Sometimes curiosity leads to nothing particularly interesting, or to an unsatisfying dead end. But if one pursues potential areas of interest sincerely and long enough, some activity or event that is personally enjoyable will invariably be found, and happiness can begin to offer its wisdom and guidance. There is no guarantee that the new club or church or activity will be an ongoing source of happiness, but the initial pleasant experience and the accompanying happiness can be the stimuli for the curious pursuit of other opportunities and an ongoing relationship with the messenger.

TRUTH AND CONSEQUENCES

People have the tendency to view happiness as the opposite of sadness, which is a disservice to both messengers. Happiness is a feeling in and of itself that appears in response to a state of well-being. It can present itself and retreat numerous times in a single day, or it can be with us for a while, only to disappear for long stretches of time.

Obviously, people have widely divergent experiences of happiness, and they pursue relationships with it in radically different ways. Some find happiness in settings of calmness and serenity, while others experience it during high-risk activities that could result in injury or death if the situation were to go awry.

Most people find happiness in situations, activities, and events that are socially acceptable, while others go outside of these boundaries, willing to face potential painful consequences for experiences that they would call happy. While many people hold common ideas about experiences that invite happiness, there is no objective standard for the messenger. A sense of well-being is purely subjective and can be identified only by the person experiencing it. When we make choices to engage in situations with the hope of experiencing happiness, we assume full responsibility for the consequences that accompany that choice. A healthy relationship with happiness can keep us mindful of the people, events, and circumstances that enrich our lives and contribute to our sense of well-being. With the guidance of this wisdom, we are free to assess the consequences of our actions and to make the choices we find to be most fulfilling.

6.

LOVE

THE MESSENGER OF SELFLESSNESS

And, in the end, the love you take
Is equal to the love you make.
—The Beatles "The End"

Ah, love! What a glorified status this messenger enjoys. People have betrayed friends, thrown away fortunes, gone to war—all in the name of this simple emotion. It is seen as a cherished prize, its pursuit framed in terms associated with combat and competition. Of all the messengers, only love is viewed as something that is won or lost. Ironically, no battle can win it, and no conquest can attain it. It cannot be claimed or owned or possessed. We can never find love when we seek it for ourselves, but the messenger is self-evident when our only thought is for the welfare of another.

THE PHYSIOLOGY OF LOVE

Love presents itself in so many forms that a simple presentation of the biological and chemical aspects of the messenger is probably impossible. Nonetheless, numerous researchers have proffered what they believe to be a biochemical basis for the emotion known as love. These theories and research studies are based upon operational definitions of love that may have a good deal to offer from an evolutionary and procreative perspective, but they do not really address love's role as a messenger and a guide in numerous other ways.

For example, when love is defined as a romantic attraction between two people, it can be seen as an emotional response eliciting an increased heart rate and pulse, an increased breathing rate, elevated blood pressure, and more rapid speech, among other "symptoms." These physiological reactions may be an accurate description of bodily changes that accompany strong attraction to another person, but by themselves they do not address the emotional experience of love.

Another operational view of love involves the notion of a chemical basis for attraction. It is believed that strong chemical messengers, known as pheromones, are produced by all animals (including humans) and discharged into the environment. Another person detects these airborne pheromones through his or her nasal receptors, and thus begins the process of chemical connection. When we strip away thousands of years of acculturation and societal development, it is easy to see the biological necessity of attraction and human bonding for the purposes of procreation and survival of the species. The notion of chemical attraction may be valid and important from a biochemical perspective, describing the primitive physiological process involved in bringing individuals together, but it does not speak to the emotional experience we call love.

Research in the field of human attachment suggests that hormonal and other biological attunement takes place between individuals in a mutually nurturing relationship, and this has been called the biological basis of love. For example, the bond between a nursing infant and a mother stimulates the release of prolactin and other hormones. This results in a calming experience for the mother while the child receives comfort and sustenance. While the bond of attachment is often a factor in the experience of love, attachment does not in and of itself guarantee the presence of the messenger.

Situations and circumstances may vary greatly, but there are times in life when the focus of one's attention is on the welfare, happiness, or needs of a person or entity other than oneself. The subjective emotional experience that accompanies this selfless regard for the other is the feeling known as love.

THIS THING CALLED LOVE

All you need is love. Love will keep us together. Love is a burning thing. Love can move mountains. If song lyrics told the whole story, one would have to think of love as the superhero of emotions—powerful, invincible, and capable of superhuman feats. In truth, love has no special powers and is rather ordinary and quite human in scope. Despite its lofty status, love presents itself only in particular situations and is no better and no worse than any of the other four messengers.

Love is the normal human feeling that accompanies an experience of selflessness. It is present during times when the feelings, needs, or welfare of another person are the primary focus or our attention. Love is not always accompanied by a joyful or even a pleasant sensation, but the attention paid to the other is always freely given without any sense of burden on the part of the giver. And while selfless attention to another is a necessary condition for love, the person giving the attention is somehow enriched by the experience. This paradoxical synergy—the enrichment and fulfillment of the giver by selfless action toward another—is why love takes its place alongside happiness as the other member of the desired duo.

Love exists along an intensity continuum ranging from mild to extreme during times of being attentive to the feelings or welfare of another person. This is somewhat more complex than the presentation of the other messengers, however, because love often accompanies other emotions. For example, concern for a friend during a medical procedure could invite the presence of love, but it might also be accompanied by the messenger fear. Taking a child to the park to play on the swings could be an activity that would allow for the experience of love, but happiness might come along for the ride. Regardless of the involvement of other emotions, the condition that allows for the subjective experience of love is the sense of selfless attention to another.

THE BIKER AND THE LAMA

Several years ago I met two people who, within twenty-four hours, gave me a lot to think about regarding the experience of love. The first meeting took place at the air pump of a gas station in Northern Virginia, though it was more of an encounter than an actual meeting. I was waiting my turn to put some air in my tires while a young man, dressed in classic biker garb, knelt next to his motorcycle adjusting the air pressure. It was a beautiful black-and-chrome bike, and the owner had obviously put a lot of time and effort into it.

"That's a beautiful bike," I said.

The biker stood up next to his motorcycle and stared straight at me. Tattooed across his forehead were the words FUCK YOU. I instinctively looked away, which I am certain was the desired effect, and the biker kick-started his motorcycle and drove off. It was a pretty weird tattoo, and an odd encounter that might have made a good cocktail party story, but the twenty-second event left me rattled and unsettled in a way I couldn't quite understand.

The very next morning I drove out to a Tibetan Buddhist temple in the Maryland countryside to hear a talk by the temple's resident lama. I had read an interesting article in the *Washington Post* about the Buddhist teacher and decided to attend one of her Sunday sermons. I don't recall very much about the rest of her talk, but at some point she was discussing what she regarded as a basic and fundamental truth: "From the nicest person you will ever meet to the most heinous criminal on death row, every human being wants exactly the same thing: they just want to be loved."

I immediately thought about the biker from the day before, and I began to wonder: If, as the lama stated, everyone wants to be loved, why would anyone put such an offensive and uninviting message on his head for the entire world to see? Who or what had hurt the biker so much that he would push people away before they ever got close enough to love him?

I have often reflected on the lama's statement about the universal desire to be cared for in a loving manner, which I myself have come to regard as a simple truth. I have also thought about the biker on a number of occasions since our brief encounter, not so much for the odd and dramatic nature of his aggressive message but for the question it brings to mind: If everyone just wants to be loved, why do so many people seem to make it so difficult to love them?

LEARNING ABOUT LOVE

Popular culture teaches us many things about love. We learn that automobiles, clothing, fast food, and a host of other products can evoke passionate love, without which our lives are somehow incomplete. We learn that love and sex are often synonymous; we learn that cunning, manipulation, and at times violent acts are required to win and secure love. It is unfortunate that pop culture is such a rotten teacher, and it is lucky for us all that what we know of love begins long before we fall victim to the appeal of marketing campaigns. Sadly, some human beings do an equally poor job preparing us to experience the messenger love.

In the chapter on happiness, I discussed Dr. Jacob Moreno's notion of the "first universe"—that is, the period of a child's earliest life in which there is no differentiation between the inside world and the outside world. Within the first universe, all experience is pure and unnamed, occurring prior to the individual's ability to conceptualize a sense of self separate and apart from others. If a child is being held and comforted, the sense of happiness the child experiences is total and complete, unrelated to any concept of being held or of another entity doing the holding or comforting. Parents and other caretakers often describe experiences like these as emotionally fulfilling bonding experiences in which they experience intense feelings of love for the child.

Does the child feel love for the parent, though? To the extent that the infant's sense of happiness and well-being incorporates the comforter into the totality of the first universe, one might call the infant's experience a raw and undirected form of love. But no matter what label one assigns to the neonatal experience of being comforted, it plays a part in allowing for the experience of love later on. Simply put, being loved paves the way to loving.

When a child is given unconditional love during his or her most vulnerable and dependent phase of life, the journey from the "all is one" reality of the first universe to the "awareness of others" in the second universe goes smoothly and without many problems. The child gradually moves into the world of objects and people with a very valuable gift in hand. That gift is the emerging sense of a self who is loved by others. A child who has been well loved begins life with a certainty about being worthwhile and valuable to others, which in time grows to a general sense of him- or herself as someone worthy of being cared for and loved. This sense of worthiness and lovability can be called "self love" and is an essential element in our later ability to love others.

Children who feel this sense of worthiness are secure in their ability to begin to explore the world around them, including the world of people. Of course, caregivers are responsible for ensuring that the child's exploration takes place within a realm of safety, but parents who love their children have little difficulty attending to this requirement. Nevertheless, not even the most alert parent can prevent visits from the vigilant triad. In the course of normal exploration, even the most secure and well-loved children will experience anger, sadness, and fear. These messengers will appear when appropriate, and loving parents and caregivers play an important role in helping the child deal with concerns associated with these feelings. When children stand on a foundation of security and worthiness that stems from the knowledge they are lovable, emotionally challenging situations do not pose a threat to their sense of self.

When children feel a sense of security in their surroundings and in themselves, their natural curiosity begins to unfold, encouraging exploration. This exploration will eventually lead them to discover and develop an interest in other people, which is the foundation of all interpersonal relationships. Curiosity about others leads to an interest in the other person's experiences and feelings. In the course of ordinary play, children will often show interest in and concern about the welfare of one another. Sharing a toy, inviting someone to participate in a game, or allowing a friend to direct a moment of play are simple, natural, and unabashed expressions of love. The child who shows a natural interest in or concern for someone else does not experience it as a burden; rather, the child expresses this interest freely and enjoys the simple pleasure that comes from helping, including, or otherwise showing concern for another person.

It would be easy to argue: "What's being described is just kids being kids; that's not love. Love is something bigger, more important, more special than that." The notion of love as a special emotion results from a number of factors, which are largely conceptual in nature. The influence of popular culture has already been touched upon, but it is clear that love is presented to us in dramatic, cartoonish, and unrealistic forms which influence our own definition of the messenger, making it appear bigger than life rather than an ordinary part of life itself. Love is associated with specific events, such as weddings or Valentine's Day, or with specific people, such as family or very close friends, which further sets it apart from ordinary everyday experience. While it is true that the intensity of the message varies depending on the circumstance or the particular person who is the object of attention, it is also true that love, like all of the emotions, presents itself in many ordinary and less intense ways.

Interest in and concern for the experiences of others is a natural by-product of the curiosity of secure and reasonably self-confident children. Nevertheless, what should be an unhampered and natural process does not come naturally to some children. Interest in others requires a temporary suspension of focus on one's own needs, and a sense of safety and security are required to create an environment that allows us that level of vulnerability. In a perfect world, all children would journey through the early years of life with a clear sense of safety and security and with an unequivocal belief that they are loved and therefore lovable. For many children, however, the world is far less than perfect.

When a child experiences abuse or neglect, concerns for safety take precedence over all other needs. Despite the limited resources available to children, they will follow the guidance of the vigilant triad to the best of their abilities to get out of harm's way when they perceive a circumstance to be threatening. Even when children are not the direct target of abuse, emotional safety is their primary concern. Aggression or violence between parents, hostility or abuse directed at a sibling, and irrational or otherwise dysfunctional behavior on the part of one or both parents are examples of situations that evoke a sense of caution and necessitate attention to personal safety and security.

When circumstances such as these are constant factors, and where love and safety are neither provided nor modeled, the notion of a relatively carefree approach to the world is too risky for a child to consider. For children raised in these situations, feeling loved and lovable will just have to wait. Without this essential security and sense of self-worth, children are not free to let down their guard enough to selflessly attend to the interests of another person. Consequently, they never experience the enjoyment that comes with loving, and they never learn that the messenger love invites us to love again.

Other early life messages can similarly make it difficult for children to experience love. When love is a frequent and welcome part of a family's emotional life, children grow up with role models who promote love as a healthy and important part of everyday experience. Some parents or caretakers, however, simply do not model love or encourage the presence of the messenger. Unresolved conflict in the marriage, resentment about being a parent, or numerous other personal or interpersonal issues can lead to an unhappy and loveless family environment. Children raised in such a setting are not exposed to love as an ordinary and easygoing messenger; they need exposure to love in other settings before they can develop a relationship with the feeling.

Some parents or caregivers set conditions for their love, which conveys to children that they are lovable only to the extent that their behavior conforms to the wishes of the adults. Thoughts, behaviors, or opinions that do not conform to the adult expectations are discouraged or punished, with no attention being paid to the distinctive qualities of the child. Of course, all caregivers must establish guidelines for children to encourage appropriate social behavior and the development of values, habits, and skills that will serve them throughout their lives. But when a focus on these expectations does not allow for an appreciation of the uniqueness and individuality of the child, unfortunate consequences result.

Children raised in these situations may conform to parental expectations and may be quite successful, but they are taught that love is a conditional emotion that is given as a reward for sanctioned behavior. The "love" they receive is not actually love at all, since it is fundamentally about the needs of the giver and not about the feelings, needs, or interests of the receiver. Conditional love has more to do with fear or a need for control than it does with selflessness.

Some parents or caregivers withhold love for another reason. They feel that too much attention to a child's unique feelings or interests will make the child conceited or egocentric, and they consciously hold back their affection and caring in the interest of what they consider appropriate parenting. This attitude promotes the notion of love as frivolous or unnecessary, and it inadvertently teaches children that love is a rare and special emotion that must be doled out carefully.

Perhaps this belief system and approach comes naturally to caregivers who have not experienced much love in their lives, or perhaps this faulty notion of appropriate parenting is passed on from one generation to the next. I can offer this observation only: While I have worked with many clients whose difficulties stemmed from a fundamental feeling of being unloved, I have *never* treated one person whose problems were caused by feeling loved too well or too much. In fact, clients who present with issues of narcissism and egocentricity are usually dealing with the wounds caused by insecurity and doubt in their own value, self-worth, and lovability. As adults, narcissistic individuals have typically developed elaborate defenses to bolster an impoverished sense of self, and they harbor a private fear of being unlovable.

I have focused a lot of attention on the influence of early learning regarding the experience of love. More than with any of the other messengers, the models and lessons learned early in life affect our access to love and its wisdom. Anger, sadness, and fear occur throughout our lives as a natural consequence of our interactions. Our assumptions, reactions, and processing of the feelings of the vigilant triad are influenced by early learning, but the messengers will present themselves to us regardless of what we have experienced or learned earlier in life. Early learning likewise influences our experience of happiness, but happiness will make at least fleeting appearances in almost everyone's life at moments of perceived well-being.

Love is the one messenger, however, that cannot appear without our consent, though our permission is often given freely and without much conscious thought. The willingness to suspend active concern for our own interests is required in order for us to create the circumstances that allow for the presence of love. When we are feeling secure, this is not a difficult process, and the enjoyable experience of love leads to the message that a focus on another individual can be personally fulfilling. In contrast, insecurity requires self-protection and is incompatible with the selflessness required for the experience of love. All children experience moments of insecurity, as do all adults. When insecurity, doubt about self-worth, and faulty messages about love begin early in life and persist into adulthood, however, the conditions required for the experience of love may never come to pass.

Many adults are unable to trust other people enough to allow themselves to be vulnerable to the degree necessary to experience love. While the roadblocks they erect may be less obvious than a tattoo on their forehead, people who are limited in their ability to trust and are wary of letting people get close to them often push people away in the interest of self-protection. This proactive rejection limits the possibility of being hurt, but it also prevents opportunities for receiving and giving love. Without access to the emotion, these adults can neither learn from the messages that love has to offer nor benefit from its wisdom. They cling to the erroneous notions of love learned in childhood and often assume cynical or other defensive postures regarding the role of love in relationships.

Nevertheless, and in spite of these self-protective strategies, such people often sense something is missing in their lives that no amount of money, accomplishment, or external reward can seem to address. Fortunately, it is never too late to learn, and the messages of childhood can be challenged, encountered, and changed to allow for the presence of love and the guidance that follows its appearance.

WATER, NOT WINE

In the process of working on this book, I shared my thoughts and ideas with many trusted colleagues and friends. Discussions about anger, sadness, fear, and happiness led to some enthusiastic dialogue that helped me flesh out my own thinking about the messengers. Everyone was pretty much on board with my basic notions about the first four feelings and the messages and guidance they offer, but the subject of love elicited spirited debate. No one had too much trouble with the connection between love and selflessness, or with the idea that love involves a satisfying feeling for the giver. The notion of love as a very ordinary emotion, however, seemed to be a sticking point, even for those who are mental health professionals. I was told that the everyday acts of selflessness may be called kindness, compassion, or just being nice, but such acts were categorically different from love.

"Love is bigger than that; it's the big kahuna of emotions," one friend said. For him, the feeling of love that people experience while caring for their own sick child or helping a family member through a hard time had little relationship to ordinary acts of thoughtfulness. My response was that while the things he described were certainly examples of love, so were helping a neighbor change a flat tire, or remembering to put down the toilet seat.

I have thought a great deal about this, and I do not claim to offer the final word on the subject, but it seems to me that love, like every other feeling, exists on a continuum of varying intensity. Kindness, compassion, or being a nice guy are simply the different words we use to describe the subjective emotional experience associated with acts of selflessness. Each messenger has its own vocabulary of descriptive words. For example, frustration, annoyance, and irritation are linguistic variants of anger; hesitation, trepidation, and terror are words associated with fear. As one of the five emotional states, love is no different, and what one person means by kindness, consideration, or thoughtfulness can never be objectively compared to another person's definition of the same word.

The variable quality in different acts of selflessness is the *intensity* of the experience of love. The emotion a person associates

LOVE: the MESSENGER of SELFLESSNESS

with the selfless regard for the welfare of his or her own child or spouse is usually much more intensely experienced than the emotion associated with taking in the neighbor's mail, but these examples of selflessness simply represent different points on the continuum of love. Like all the messengers, love breathes, expanding and contracting in intensity according to different circumstances and different people. Intensity also varies with feelings for the same person in different settings or at different times. We might have a general sense of love for another person, but the intensity or subjective strength of the feeling never remains totally constant over time. There are even times when our concern or focus of attention does not invite selflessness, and our feelings of love for someone we feel close to may be temporarily off the radar screen.

If it is true that love is as ordinary as any of the other messengers, then why do so many people regard it as an emotion in a class by itself? To answer this question we must consider the vulnerability required to achieve the intimacy associated with intense, strongly experienced love between people. All acts of love, from the most ordinary to the most extraordinary, are selfless acts that enrich the person who attends to another individual. As previously discussed, all selflessness requires vulnerability, and temporary disregard for one's own interests leaves a person exposed to potential hurt.

There is a direct correlation between the level of the vulnerability and the intensity of the intimacy: greater intensity requires greater vulnerability. When we love intensely and deeply, we are also intensely and deeply vulnerable to being hurt. One could say that love is risky business, but the strength and intensity of the personal fulfillment that comes with deep love is worth the risk to the one who loves. It is this unique quality of self-imposed vulnerability that contributes to the notion of love as a separate and "bigger" emotion, for no other messenger requires great exposure to potential hurt in exchange for great reward.

Even though the intense and strongly experienced variety of

love represents the extreme point on the continuum, people tend to focus on this limited viewpoint when they define love. When seen in this light, love is like some rare, fine wine that should be handled delicately and reserved for some special event. If we consider the entire spectrum of love, however, we can see that the fulfilling experience of selflessness can enrich us in many less intense, more ordinary, and everyday ways. From this perspective, love is not a rare wine; rather, it is more analogous to water—necessary to sustain us and readily available.

LOVE, SEX, AND ROMANCE

The pairing of love and sex is part of the fabric of our culture. It is the theme of countless movies, TV shows, plays, and songs, and it is promoted on the covers of many magazines that line the supermarket checkout lines. Sex is just one of the countless ways love can be expressed and experienced, but it receives so much attention that one could easily believe love cannot exist without sex. Of course, the experience of love has nothing to do with sex per se, though it is often a factor in romantic relationships that include sex.

Sexual behavior between consenting adults can be exciting and fun, but it does not automatically involve love. Sex has the *potential* for being an intimate form of physical connection between people, but it is not *necessarily* intimate. The selfless attention to the interests of another is the defining characteristic of all love, and this is the case with love that is expressed sexually as well. When the main focus of a sexual encounter involves achieving one's own sexual satisfaction, a mutually satisfying experience may result, but it is not an expression of mutual love—it is primarily about having sex. When a couple engages in sex with selfless regard for the needs and pleasure of one another, the experience can truly be called making love.

I am not assigning a moral judgment to having sex vs. making love, nor am I suggesting that one expression of sex is more pleasurable than the other. Many couples who have deep feelings of love for one another have sex lives that are less than satisfying, and people who feel no particular love for one another can have satisfying sexual experiences. Our culture regards sex as a secretive and taboo behavior, which gives the false impression that it is automatically intimate as well. The important point in this discussion is that despite what we are led to believe by the messages of our culture, sex and love are not the same thing.

In romantic relationships, some individuals make a very big distinction between loving someone and being *in* love. This point is usually underscored when one member of a couple has decided to leave the relationship. The notion of loving or being in love may have different meanings to different people, but it is usually a matter of declining intensity of feeling. When people say that they love, but are no longer in love with, another person, they are usually saying that their regard for the other person does not evoke the level of excitement or satisfaction that it once did.

The pain associated with the unwanted end of a romantic relationship has the potential of making someone wary of future opportunities to experience love. But with time and the nonromantic expressions of love that come from the support of friends and family, most people eventually decide the fulfillment that accompanies a romantic relationship involving mutual love is worth the risk. Unwilling to live without it, they set out to love again.

Jack and Hannah

When Jack and Hannah met in college, their strong initial attraction to each other paved the way for the loving relationship that followed. They shared many interests and delighted in the opportunity to spend time in each other's company. They introduced each other to new experiences, new opportunities, and new people, adding quality and richness to both their lives. Every new bit of information was embraced with fascination and curiosity, and they looked forward to each opportunity to learn more about the other. As Jack and Hannah's mutual interest continued to grow, so did their desire to contribute to each other's happiness. Opportunities to show thoughtfulness and caring were never experienced as burdensome; the warmth and satisfaction each of them felt made kindness its own reward. The marriage vows they exchanged shortly after graduation were sincerely spoken, as was the promise to love each other to the end of their days.

Twenty years later Jack and Hannah sat in my office uncertain about the future of their relationship. The tension and defensiveness surrounding them was like a thick fog that clouded their vision and affected all their interactions with each other. The interest, affection, and concern that were once a routine part of their relationship had been replaced with resentment, distain, and growing distance from one another. Both Jack and Hannah saw themselves as victims of the other's insensitivity and selfishness, and each of them held the other responsible for the decline of the relationship. Couples therapy was seen as a last-ditch effort to salvage the marriage, and neither of them was particularly optimistic about the possibility of the marriage being saved. The love they had apparently experienced in abundance in the early years of their relationship was nowhere to be found.

By the time couples reach this stage in a relationship it is often too late to repair the damage. Typically, one or both of the spouses have already decided to leave. They may have privately reached the decision that they no longer want to live with the daily unhappiness, and they do not want to put the effort into trying to recapture what by now has become a vague memory of a loving relationship. They may have already begun a new relationship, which feels more fulfilling, or they are simply no longer interested in their spouse's feelings or concerns, preferring a life alone to the daily lack of a satisfying emotional connection. In any event, when all desire to attend to the interests of the other person is gone, there is little any couples therapist can do to breathe life into the relationship.

So how does a loving, supportive, and caring relationship devolve to such an unhappy and unfulfilling state? It generally occurs as a slow, steady decline over a long period of time, as was the case with Jack and Hannah. There were many joys and a number of stressful events over the course of their marriage, as occur in the course of any relationship. Much of their married life had centered on raising their son, who was now a freshman at college. They rejoiced in his accomplishments and fretted over his challenges, but overall they were quite happy with the fine young man they had lovingly guided into adulthood.

Shortly after their son was born, Hannah was diagnosed with cancer, which required surgery, chemotherapy, and a number of years of follow-up treatment before it was declared cured. A few years later, Jack lost his job when his company folded, and he was unemployed for the better part of a year. Following some financially insecure months, he landed a new and better job and had been employed ever since. These major life difficulties were certainly stressful, but in and of themselves they did not account for the couple's growing distance and eventual lack of love. Somewhere along the way, Jack and Hannah stopped caring about what the other one thought, felt, or desired. Selflessness had been replaced by self-protection; they felt wounded by one another, and the resentment that followed colored their perception of the person they had married and pushed the possibility of love further and further away.

An objective assessment of how and when their affection began to wane would have been impossible. The resentment and perceived victimization each of them harbored toward the other allowed for only finger-pointing and accusations. Jack felt the problems in the relationship were clearly Hannah's fault, and vice versa. I felt more like a referee than a therapist, and my efforts to facilitate a civil discussion of their individual perceptions of the problem were futile. When Jack had the floor, he used it as an opportunity to present evidence against Hannah, and she just rolled her eyes, drummed her fingers, and could barely wait to mount a defense and launch her own attack. Then the scene was repeated in the reverse. Each was not only unable to speak about his or her own experiences but also, more important, each was unable to truly listen to the other.

There are a number of different approaches to working with couples, but all of them focus on communication as the essential vehicle for change. Effective communication requires both an ability to present one's viewpoint in a way that can be understood by another person and an ability to truly hear what is being said. In couples therapy, honest, non-defensive communication allows for a better understanding of the other person, but it does not guarantee that the relationship will stay intact. Sometimes, effective communication leads to an honest appreciation that two people have grown in different directions and no longer want to stay together.

I had no way of knowing the eventual outcome of Jack and Hannah's situation, but it was obvious no real communication was taking place. After collecting what background information I could, and trying to establish some basic ground rules, I recommended the following homework assignment: Prior to the next session, Jack and Hannah were to find three ten-minute blocks of time when they would be free of distractions or interruptions. For the first five minutes of each session, one of them was to talk about some personal experience. They were not allowed to talk about the relationship, about the other person, or about areas of perceived conflict; they were to tell the other person anything they wanted about themselves while steering clear of any emotionally charged topics. They could talk about something as innocuous as a pet they had as a child, a class they enjoyed in school, or some hobby they wished to pursue. The person who was not talking was asked to practice listening to the other person. The listener was not to interrupt, disagree, or add his or her own thoughts to the mix, but could ask for more information if he or she was either uncertain about what was meant or wanted to know more about what was being said. At the end of five minutes they were to switch places, the speaker now being the listener and following the same guidelines.

The homework sounds simple enough, but I have given the same assignment to many couples and they rarely attempt it, let alone complete it before the next session. Jack and Hannah came to their next session with a number of excuses for why they couldn't find thirty minutes during the week to work on the relationship, and then they proceeded to try to draw me into the referee role once again. One might think the desperate state of the relationship would compel a couple to try anything that might help, but such is not the case.

I used their noncompliance to underscore the important point that Jack and Hannah were so entrenched in their own defensive positions, they were unwilling to drop their guards long enough to connect with one another. Neither one of them trusted the other person to listen without a defensive attack, so neither of them was willing to risk revealing anything personal, however superficial it might be. This initial effort to reestablish a pathway for communication had to take place in the therapy session itself. I facilitated the speaking and listening process, providing feedback and gentle guidance when the process strayed from the simple task of honest talking and sincere listening.

The initial focus on safe, seemingly superficial material allowed two important things to take place. First, Jack and Hannah were able to talk about themselves and their own feelings without blaming or accusing one another. Second, the one who was doing the listening was able to rediscover something that had been missing from the relationship for a very long time: namely, curiosity and interest in the other. Of course, curiosity and interest are not the same thing as love, but without interest there is no possibility for caring, concern, or love. Fortunately, the renewed spark of interest in one another was a welcome relief from the hostility that had marked their relationship, and it reminded each of them of a time in the relationship when love was easy to give and receive.

With a renewed interest in each other's view of things, Jack and Hannah gradually took on more challenging levels of communication. An honest willingness to try to appreciate the other person's unhappiness led to more difficult and more productive talk. Somewhat of a breakthrough in therapy came when they talked about the feelings they had had around the time of her cancer treatment and his unemployment. Jack talked about the fear he felt when Hannah was sick, but how he never expressed his fear out of respect for what he saw as her stoic approach to the disease. Hannah revealed her own terror about the cancer, but she assumed a tough exterior so as not to frighten their son. She admitted that she harbored some anger at what she saw as Jack's indifference to her health, unaware that he was desperately frightened of losing her.

A similar dynamic occurred around the period of Jack's unemployment. His air of indifference about being unemployed masked his anger and sadness about the failure of his company and his fear about reentering the job market. Hannah had been angry about what she assumed was a lack of concern for their financial well-being, but she didn't want to express her feelings for fear of appearing unsupportive. Anger, sadness, and fear—these messengers were practically screaming to be listened to, but false assumptions and an unwillingness to risk rejection pushed Jack and Hannah apart rather than bringing them together at their times of greatest need. The messenger love was lost in the confusion.

Jack and Hannah's problems were not caused by some misconceptions around a time of crisis. Somewhere along the way they developed the habit of not addressing difficult or unpleasant feelings when they arose. In the early part of their relationship, they could easily experience the love of sharing a favorite poem, but they failed to see that love could also be present in a discussion about the annoyance of someone forgetting to refill the ice cube tray. In any relationship, when someone believes it is not worth the hassle to address some perceived slight or hurt or annoyance, that person is greasing the skids for love to slip away.

People sometimes tell themselves the "small stuff" is not important, but the truth is that an unwillingness to deal with the small stuff makes it harder to address more substantial issues when they arise. Mutual love requires a commitment to sharing feelings, which is easy when the feeling is happiness but more difficult when the feelings of the vigilant triad are concerned. Talking about things that bug us can be accomplished with regard for the other person's feelings, but it feels safe to express our concerns only when we believe the other person cares. This kind of exchange may not seem particularly romantic, but it is the kind of expression of love that sustains and strengthens relationships.

Jack and Hannah continued to work on honest communication, which involved both talking and listening with sincere regard for the other person. The work involved taking the risk of speaking about their own models for communication, their expectations about the marriage, their hopes, their disappointments, their wishes, and their fears. They eventually rediscovered that when communication is approached with heartfelt regard for the other person, love is self-evident. The intensity and depth of that love is a matter of subjective experience, and only the person who feels the love can say whether or not it is enough to sustain an ongoing relationship or to restore a marriage. Fortunately for Jack and Hannah, it was not too late.

PRACTICING LOVE

In a later chapter I offer some suggestions for developing stronger relationships with the five messengers, but let me simply assert in the conclusion to this chapter that strengthening anything requires practice. For anyone who wants to learn more about love, there are abundant opportunities to practice. Nonetheless, while the message love offers is one of satisfaction and encouragement to love again, many people choose to neglect or avoid opportunities to practice behaviors that invite love. Some people are unwilling to move beyond a familiar space of attention to their own needs, which offers a safe brand of complacency. For others, the need for safety and security prohibits even the most primitive efforts at selflessness. These individuals want the safety and security of being loved, yet they are unwilling or unable to offer love until they get it. The self-protective walls they erect often push people away, decreasing the opportunities for getting the love they want, leading to a self-fulfilling cycle that is like a snake eating its own tail!

In therapy, clients often need to learn how to relax their defenses in order to create a hospitable environment for love. The late writer and psychotherapist Sheldon Kopp reportedly once said that he approached psychotherapy by trying to love his clients, then helping them understand why they would not let him. For individuals who have difficulty letting down their guard, some preparatory work may be necessary, but sooner or later, learning about love comes down to taking a risk. As with all the messengers, cultivating a relationship with love is easier at the low end of the intensity spectrum. It would be absurd to suggest that someone should learn about fear by jumping out of an airplane, and it would be just as foolish for someone to dive headlong into a committed relationship to try to learn about love.

When people are ready and willing, the opportunities to experience love are everywhere. Any act of kindness or assistance, when offered sincerely and with an eye toward the needs of another person, creates a moment of selflessness and allows for the appearance of love. Holding the door for a stranger, helping a friend with a chore, assisting a child with homework are all ordinary examples of acts of selflessness. Attending to the feelings that accompany these gestures is the way to become more familiar with the everyday possibilities for love. Volunteering to support some community activity or charitable cause could provide a more formal opportunity for selfless action and the presence of love. For many people, gestures such as these are a routine part of their lives, and they take for granted the satisfaction that accompanies their volunteerism. Whether someone practices selflessness as a customary part of daily life or in an effort to explore new and unfamiliar territory, attention to the accompanying feeling is how the wisdom and messages of love are made conscious and available.

In one way, the message of love is no different from the messages of any of the other feelings: it is always a personal message for the one who experiences it, and it invites reflection and consideration of the choices we make in our own best interest. As a member of the desired duo, love tastes like more, but how a person responds to his or her tingling taste buds is a matter of personal choice. Love might inspire further acts of selflessness or stimulate creative pursuits, or it may simply be experienced as a satisfying moment in and of itself. Love has been a major messenger in career choices for many people in the helping professions, but it is certainly not the only motivating emotion; many people who have chosen careers in business and industry are more compassionate and selfless than many professional helpers. When we are attentive to love, the messenger offers the wisdom and guidance necessary to help us mindfully evaluate our options and follow the path that makes the most sense to us.

AMOR VINCIT OMNIA

I remember very little of my high school Latin, but I do recall the phrase *amor vincit omnia*—love conquers all. It is a lovely sentiment, but love alone does not address all things, of course, nor is it any more important or more valuable than any of the other messengers. Sometimes, attention to the other feelings is immediate and more appropriate; at such times a healthy relationship with the vigilant triad allows for the sense of security that makes love possible.

The wisdom and guidance of love can inspire us to look out for the interests of one another, which would certainly promote peaceful and harmonious relationships. It is the essence of the Golden Rule and the teaching of all great religions that we should practice charity and compassion and treat other people the way we want to be treated. Sometimes, love and devotion are sincerely felt for groups, institutions, or spirituality, emanating from the same selfless regard that allows for the presence of love between individuals. Sincerely held patriotism, dedication to a cause, and devotion to God are examples of selflessness that invite the presence of love.

If everyone subscribed to the same notion of selfless regard for others, our safety, security, and well-being would be a reality of community living. By extension, concern for our neighbor would assure the end of war, hunger, and misery throughout the world. Apparently, that is just not the present story of the human race. If you ask any child to break a candy bar in two and give half to a friend, he or she will invariably give the smaller portion to the friend. It would appear that kindness, charity, and selflessness are not innate and must be learned and practiced before their value is revealed to us. Love is an important part of this process, because the satisfaction and enjoyment that accompany acts of selflessness compel us to seek out more opportunities to love. When love becomes a routine part of everyday life, listening to its message and following its guidance are natural and uncomplicated.

FINDING BALANCE IN THE STORM

There's no secret to balance. You just have to ride the waves.
—Frank Herbert

A good deal of my motivation for writing this book came from my work with clients in psychotherapy sessions. Psychotherapy often focuses on people's misconceptions about what feelings are and their difficulties with appreciating emotions as normal responses to their environment. Establishing or restoring a healthy, balanced appreciation of normal human emotion is critical before feelings can be relied upon as messengers and guides. There are a number of different approaches to psychotherapy, but in its own way each approach attempts to help individuals establish a comfortable working relationship with emotions.

Insight-oriented psychotherapy approaches this goal by helping clients develop their conscious awareness of the intrapsychic forces contributing to the patterns and choices that are causing pain in their present lives. This approach holds that insight can help individuals release the grip of unconscious processes and allow the opportunity for change. The feelings associated with the material discussed in insight-oriented psychotherapy are important to people developing an awareness of their own internal road map and in building an honest emotional life, free of unconscious, habitual, and self-defeating patterns.

In contrast to the insight-oriented approach, behavior therapy focuses on present-day patterns of behavior and attempts to change a person's response to emotionally challenging situations. Behavior therapy contends that when we change the way we respond to situations that create emotional difficulty, the emotional experience follows suit. The intensity of emotional discomfort experienced in a particular situation, for example, can become less debilitating when healthy responses to the challenging situation are learned and practiced.

A popular third approach to psychotherapy is cognitive therapy, which focuses on clients' thought processes to address emotional concerns. This approach asserts that symptoms of emotional discomfort are caused by patterns of thinking that create an inaccurate and unhealthy internal picture, which further results in undesired emotional responses. Cognitive therapists try to teach clients to replace the maladaptive thought patterns with healthier thought patterns to engender more emotional harmony.

Practitioners of the different schools of psychotherapy will often vehemently defend their particular approach and are sometimes quite critical of the other forms of treatment. In truth, each approach can point to treatment successes, and the approach that works best for one client might not feel comfortable to another client. The formation of a solid therapeutic relationship with a knowledgeable and skilled therapist seems to cut across all approaches as the most important factor in creating an environment for psychological growth. What each of these divergent schools of thought recognizes is that a person's emotional experience of the world is the final measure of whether he or she has been helped by treatment. Clients who end psychotherapy with a satisfying relationship with their own emotions will consider the treatment a success, regardless of the particular approach.

While I certainly hope this book will be helpful to therapy clients, I did not specifically write it for individuals who are either considering or currently engaged in psychotherapy. *The Wisdom of the Five Messengers* offers guidance for all people, in life situations ranging from the most ordinary to the most stressful. Sometimes the intensity of someone's emotional experience makes it difficult for him or her to attend to these messages, and some professional help is needed. When men and women enter into psychotherapy it is typically because they are having difficulty with one or more emotional states that are causing discomfort and possibly dysfunction.

Occasionally, people seek treatment because their behavior is causing emotional discomfort for others, as in the case of a child who is getting into trouble with drugs or alcohol, or a spouse whose extramarital affair has been discovered. Unless these clients acknowledge some level of personal emotional pain around the behavior that is upsetting their loved ones, however, there is little that psychotherapy has to offer. The wounded parent or spouse would be more likely to benefit from counseling or psychotherapy.

All discomfort is a personal experience, and an objective comparison of the emotional pain of different individuals is impossible. Nevertheless, many people endure or suffer intense emotional discomfort that would compel others in similar circumstances to seek mental health treatment. Intensely uncomfortable emotional experiences, even those that last for a prolonged period of time, become diagnosed clinical conditions only when someone assigns a diagnosis to them. The difference between diagnosed clinical conditions and everyday presentations of the messengers is in many cases a matter of the emotional intensity of the experience and the subjective degree of discomfort.

Remember the fuse box? Human beings appear to have differing predispositions toward emotions that become taxed or overburdened at times of stress. Aggression, depression, and panic are expressions of overburdened circuits that interfere with a healthy relationship with the messengers. Further on in this chapter I present some of the common issues and concerns for which clients seek treatment to show how feelings manifest in the clinical arena and to discuss some of the challenges these conditions pose to establishing a healthy relationship with the messengers. It is important to bear in mind at this juncture, however, that a healthy relationship with the five messengers is of benefit to all individuals, not just those who seek treatment, and that emotional pain is a subjective experience. Many people who never seek professional help have a satisfying emotional life, while others move through life with a constant level of discomfort. It is also important to understand that subjective emotional experience varies greatly within clinical categories: for example, depression does not always involve suicidal thinking, and anxiety does not always involve panic attacks.

DIAGNOSIS AND EXPERIENCE

The Diagnostic and Statistical Manual of Mental Disorders, Fourth Edition (hereafter referred to simply as the DSM-IV) is published by the American Psychiatric Association and is the standard diagnostic manual used in the mental health professions. The DSM-IV assigns specific diagnoses to symptoms to provide a uniform way of identifying problems of an emotional nature. It is a valuable tool for assigning an agreed-upon label to a set of symptoms, which is important for communication among professionals and for research purposes. As I stated previously, however, emotional discomfort is ultimately subjective, and no label can truly communicate the personal experience of the diagnosis. Additionally, emotional discomfort cannot always be easily identified with a single diagnosis and may involve features of differing diagnoses. Nonetheless, diagnostic descriptions provide a helpful language for discussing emotional concerns, and each diagnosis can be discussed in terms of its relationship to one or more of the five messengers.

The DSM-IV contains more than three hundred diagnostic descriptions, and a discussion of the relationship between each diagnosis and the five messengers is beyond the scope of this book. Rather, I have chosen to present some of the common clinical issues that compel people to seek the help of a mental health professional and to talk about the challenges involved in allowing the five messengers to reveal themselves in a useful form. I have selected these particular concerns with the belief that all readers, including those who have never engaged in formal counseling or psychotherapy, will be able to relate to and benefit from the issues discussed.

Anxiety

As a clinical issue as well as in the popular use of the word, anxiety involves the messenger fear. When someone speaks of being anxious about an important meeting, a public speaking engagement, or financial matters, he or she is typically referring to concerns about unknown consequences that might be associated with these events. As I have discussed, fear is the messenger of the unknown and alerts us to concerns about unwanted outcomes of our actions. When we are able to attend to fear and mindfully consider its messages, we can usually get through the anxious event, often with a sense of accomplishment or success.

Anxiety disorders are among the most common emotional disturbances. An estimated 19 million Americans suffer from anxiety disorders, and nearly one-third of all Americans will have at least one panic attack at some time in their lives. Fear is present when someone is experiencing a panic attack or a highly anxious state, but the overwhelming nature of the experience makes it impossible for anyone to attend mindfully to fear as a messenger and guide. During a panic attack or a highly anxious state, the individual is usually focused on the uncomfortable physical symptoms—the racing heart, the shortness of breath, and so forth—which puts in motion a self-perpetuating cycle of anxiety about the symptoms, which creates more anxiety. This fear of fear fuels the panic and prevents any productive communication with the messenger. Simply put, a person having a panic attack just wants it to go away.

When overwhelming symptoms prevent us from following the guidance of the messengers, symptom relief is needed before the feelings can be appreciated as something other than the enemy. Antianxiety medication can be helpful in this regard, but the use of this medication in treating anxiety disorders presents an interesting paradox. People who are highly anxious are often fearful of losing control, and they tend to see the use of medication as a surrender of control to some chemical agent. Thus, the people who could most benefit from antianxiety medication are often the most resistant to using it for symptom relief. Education and reassurance are often helpful, and a number of behavioral psychology approaches—including relaxation training, grounding techniques, and redirection—can help provide nonchemical symptom relief. In the case of a specific phobia, systematic desensitization techniques are often effective in helping to reduce anxiety and to restore a sense of control.

When clients experience relief from the extreme discomfort of their anxiety symptoms, they are often eager to end treatment and resume their prior life. They regard the anxiety or panic as a disruption to their normal sense of control and want to believe they have forever excised it from their lives. In many ways, however, symptom relief merely clears the way for the real work to begin. Answering the questions "Why did I experience this disruption to my sense of control?" and "What caused the anxiety attack?" requires spending time with the messenger fear—and often other messengers as well—which can be accomplished only once the symptoms are not experienced as overwhelming.

The course of psychotherapy usually addresses the perceived need to control strong emotions and attempts to help clients appreciate, rather than avoid, their feelings. Clients often have particular difficulty accepting their own anger, but fear of all strongly held emotions is at the core of most anxiety disorders. Once the overwhelming symptoms of anxiety are brought under control, the client is ready to begin to address the fear associated with intensely experienced emotions. When fear can be seen and appreciated as a valued messenger and guide, not as an enemy, people can begin to address the real and uniquely personal issues that drive their anxiety, and they can start to consider more satisfying ways of expressing strong emotions.

Depression

Clinical depression involves many of the features traditionally associated with sadness. Tearfulness, lack of interest, and a general slowing down of one's response to the world are not uncommon reactions when someone experiences significant loss, which invites the presence of sadness. As discussed in the chapter on sadness, the difference between sadness and clinical depression is a matter of degree and longevity. As a messenger, sadness offers us the opportunity to appreciate the significance of what has been lost and to make mindful choices about how to proceed beyond the loss. The experience of sadness changes over time and gradually runs its course, allowing for the presence of other messengers.

Clinical depression sometimes, but not always, begins with an experience of loss, but the sadness that loss evokes does not lift, and often deepens long after the initial loss. Unlike sadness, clinical depression appears to take on a life of its own, usually marked by a sense of helplessness and hopelessness, which frequently involves suicidal thoughts and ideas. The bleak overlay that depression brings to a person's view of the world makes it impossible to attend to sadness as a useful and helpful messenger. In the midst of a depressive episode, the intensity of the discomfort typically prevents clients from being able to consider choices that could lead to more comfort in the future.

Sadness is not the only messenger that is blocked by clinical depression. Obviously, when someone is depressed, happiness cannot be seen or appreciated, and the intense self-absorption of the condition prevents the appearance of love as well. The strength and wisdom of anger, which can offer guidance related to making choices to address perceived unfairness, is also hidden from view. In this regard, it is notable that depression is often conceptualized as anger turned inward and is experienced many times as harsh self-judgment.

As with anxiety, medication can be helpful in providing relief from the overwhelming symptoms of depression, and it is often part of the overall treatment. Without some relief from the dreary and hopeless worldview that accompanies severe depression, clients are often unable to benefit from self-exploration, and they have difficulty following through on behavioral or cognitive homework suggestions. But without some understanding of the dynamics and circumstances that have contributed to the sense of a downward spiral, clients are likely to revert to patterns and roles that lead to a recurring experience of depression. Research has shown that a combination of antidepressant medication and psychotherapy is generally the best approach to dealing with clinical depression.

After stability and safety have been established, clients who remain in treatment can embark on the same healing journey that is at the heart of all psychotherapy: the establishment of a healthy and respectful relationship with one's own feelings. With a sincere commitment to the healing process, sadness can be appreciated as a messenger and guide and can be seen as something quite different from the stuck despondency of depression.

Anger Management

When their impulsive displays of irrational aggression or violence are a concern, people usually seek some form of anger management therapy. As discussed in the chapter on anger, the very term "anger management" is a misnomer. "Aggressive behavior management therapy" would be a more accurate and appropriate name for the treatment because the messenger anger is a feeling, not the troublesome behavior that causes concern.

Impulsive aggressive responses occur in many different settings, from casual encounters in parking lots and supermarkets to more personal interactions in the workplace and in the home. A perception of injustice and an initial feeling of anger always stimulate these responses, but the quick and aggressive reaction that follows the feeling occurs with a swiftness and an intensity that make it impossible to attend to anger as a messenger and guide.

Impulsive and destructive responses to anger can be effectively treated in psychotherapy, but the question of motivation often comes into play. Some people who display uncontrolled aggressive responses to perceived injustice have trouble seeing their own behavior as unjustified. They tend to frame their responses as logical and appropriate reactions to other people's unfair treatment of them. Minor traffic altercations, criticism from a boss or a coworker, or disagreements in social settings are seen as outrageous violations that justify aggressive action. In the home, this dynamic is at the root of domestic violence in which an abuser blames the spouse for causing the out-of-control behavior. When responses to anger take a violent form, the law may get involved, and many referrals for anger management therapy are court ordered or sought at the advice of a lawyer who is preparing a defense. If the clients privately believe their behavior is justified, it is unlikely they will derive much benefit from treatment. It brings to mind the old joke, "How many therapists does it take to change a lightbulb?" The answer is, "Only one, but the lightbulb really has to want to change."

Substance abuse also contributes to the problem of impulsive aggressive behavior. Drugs and alcohol often lower inhibitions and impair judgment, which makes a situation of perceived injustice potentially volatile. It is not mere coincidence that substance-impaired individuals commit the overwhelming percentage of homicides.

Nonetheless, many people who are prone toward impulsive aggression recognize that their behavior is inappropriate, that it causes pain and suffering for people they care about, and that it negatively affects their lives. When someone sincerely wants to change, help is available. While medication can sometimes address underlying anxiety or agitated depression, there is no "anti-aggression" pill to prevent impulsive aggressive responses. Forging a healthy relationship with anger is the key to changing one's responses to perceived injustice.

Various approaches to therapy can help a person develop nonaggressive responses to circumstances that are seen as unfair or unjust. Most approaches begin by attempting to change the automatic aggressive response by stopping or interrupting the rapid sequence of thoughts that lead to the unwanted behavior. People learn to recognize the precursors to their aggressive response and to take action to head off the response before it escalates into undesired behavior. For individuals prone toward aggressive reactions, the challenge involves being able to recognize, appreciate, and respond to anger at the low end of the spectrum, before it manifests as rage. Mild annoyance, inconvenience, and frustration are all variants of anger, and these need to be attended to before they take on unwieldy proportions.

Many people who know how to express their rage, however, know very little about expressing anger in these more ordinary and everyday forms. An important part of therapy involves learning to identify these variants of anger and developing forms of expression that demand respect for one's own rights without violating the rights of others. This is the very guidance the messenger anger offers: namely, the opportunity to clearly assess the nature and impact of perceived injustice and to address these issues with the personal choices that are in one's best interest.

Once reactive aggression is under control and a healthy relationship with anger has begun, clients in therapy usually discover that other feelings are involved in their aggressive approach. The active quality of aggression is sometimes erroneously seen as the opposite of fear, which is regarded as a weakness. Fear of being hurt or of being out of control often stimulates an inappropriate episode of aggression. Likewise, sadness related to loss of status, loss of opportunity, or loss of relationships, among other losses, is often regarded as a weakness, which the false strength of aggression attempts to control. As with all the issues that bring clients to seek treatment, eventually an invitation is extended to learn from the wisdom and guidance of all the messengers.

Relationship Issues

Another common reason why people seek therapy is to address problems in a marriage or some other relationship. Sometimes a client seeks individual therapy with the intention of learning how to "fix" his or her spouse. The treatment either changes to include both members of the relationship in couples counseling, or the client must abandon the notion of trying to change a spouse in absentia and begin to focus on his or her own feelings for guidance in dealing with the unsatisfactory relationship.

The physical presence of both members of a couple is still not enough if one or both of them are not really interested in changing things or are no longer interested in saving the relationship. When both members of a couple are willing to work on addressing problems in the relationship, however, counseling can help. The case of Jack and Hannah in the chapter on love touches on the essential element in all approaches to couples therapy—communication. With the many changes that occur in the course of any relationship, some couples lose their original commitment to talking about and listening to each other's thoughts, dreams, and issues. Some couples have never had any such commitment. They have approached the relationship with very different expectations, goals, and concerns, which can eventually reach a point of conflict. Restoring or establishing healthy communication is the only real hope for sustainable satisfaction in a relationship.

One might ask, "Communication about what?" The answer is anything and everything, but primarily communication must be about feelings. A healthy relationship with ourselves that fosters growth requires us to attend to our feelings, to listen to their messages, and to follow their guidance. A healthy relationship with another person in which both parties grow requires that we not only attend to our own messengers but also to the messengers of the other person. Each person must take responsibility for his or her own feelings, but the health of a relationship requires couples to develop a style of communication that also allows both partners to honestly share their feelings.

The beauty of relationships is that no two are exactly alike, and each couple must create their own unique way of attending to one another's emotions. The common elements generally required among all couples, however, are trust, honesty, and a sincere regard for the feelings of the other person. Often, couples therapy must address old patterns, past hurts, and defensive posturing, among other factors, before trust, honesty, and thoughtfulness are present in the relationship. As stated previously, intimacy and vulnerability are one and the same, and intimate relationships require an investment in understanding and appreciating how the five messengers speak to and guide the person we are intimate with. In healthy relationships, feelings are freely expressed, and people feel comfortable and secure in the belief their feelings will be handled with care.

Sometimes couples need to learn the difference between truth and honesty. Truth is a straightforward presentation of the facts, as they are perceived. Honesty is a communication of that truth in a way that honors the relationship. What we say and how we say it both matter. When people approach the people they care about with honesty, even the most difficult emotional discussions can add to the strength and quality of the relationship.

Parenting Concerns

Frustration with issues related to raising children is another common stimulus for seeking the help of a therapist. Children and adolescents often struggle with issues of adjustment, identity, and socialization that sometimes require the help of a mental health professional. In an important way, the challenges facing children with emotional concerns are no different from the challenges that adults face. Ultimately, the ability to attend to one's own feelings and to use the guidance that follows to make healthy choices is the essence of mental balance for everyone, children and adults alike. The wisdom and guidance of the five messengers are easier to follow when a healthy relationship with feelings has been established in childhood.

The stress and demands of childhood and adolescence are formidable, however, and conflict with parents and caregivers is inevitable. When parents seek the help of a therapist to address issues regarding their children, their concerns are usually behavioral in nature. Academic problems, oppositional behavior, antisocial acts, or substance abuse are among the more common concerns for which parents seek assistance. Effective intervention often involves a holistic response to the child's problem, requiring a coordination of efforts among the parents and other involved adults. Depending upon the nature of the concern, teachers, counselors, and at times police or officers of the court may need to be involved. Although parents need to be informed about available resources and sometimes need to be educated about effective parenting methods, changing problem behaviors eventually boils down to an ability and a willingness to set clear and consistent expectations and a commitment to establishing and following through on reasonable consequences.

Here's where the messengers come into play. When dealing with concerns about their children, parents sometimes have difficulty attending to their own feelings. Emotions tend to be experienced with intensity, particularly as problem behaviors escalate, which makes it difficult to mindfully consider one's feelings. When parents address significant concerns regarding their children, the messengers of the vigilant triad are usually present. Anger about the sense of unfairness, sadness about change and loss, and fear about the unknown future are typically part of any parenting crisis, but the intensity of the emotions and the need to respond quickly to a perceived emergency make it very difficult for parents to attend to the vigilant triad for guidance. Additionally, the love that most parents have for their children is often severely tested when efforts to help the child are rejected or sabotaged. The unique emotional history of family interactions often complicates the picture, making it difficult for parents to evaluate their own present-day feelings without filtering them through the lens of the past.

Ultimately, any reasoned response to a child's difficulties must involve the feelings of the parents. The suggestions and guidance of well-meaning therapists, teachers, or friends are just that—suggestions and guidance. Parents must come to terms with an approach that makes the most sense to them regarding the welfare of their children, which requires an honest acceptance of all the feelings involved. If an otherwise well-adjusted child is struggling with one subject at school, the remedy requiring parental involvement might be relatively uncomplicated. With more complex issues, such as an academically failing, substance-abusing child who refuses to acknowledge a problem, a clear approach to the situation may be more difficult.

Nonetheless, whether the problem is simple or complex, parents must live with the consequences of their decisions, and their own feelings offer guidance for making good choices even in bad situations. Counseling or psychotherapy can help parents sort through the confusing wash of mixed emotions and can help them address the issues that may be preventing them from honestly accepting their own feelings. In the end, setting and enforcing rules and consequences, interacting with other involved adults, and generally doing the often-difficult work of effective parenting is easier to accomplish when the actions parents take are consistent with what they feel.

Once an identified problem has been resolved, the messengers continue to be important in the relationship between parents and children. The course of treatment involved in more complex issues, such as substance abuse or legal problems, usually requires family counseling to improve the communication among family members. As with any relationship, healthy family relationships require an environment in which each member can express his or her individual feelings, and they require a commitment by everyone to try to appreciate and understand the feelings of other members of the family. Honesty, respect, and acceptance are important elements of this kind of environment, and hard work is usually required to establish and maintain it. While the feelings of all family members are important, family relationships differ from couples' relationships in one crucial way: the parents are the final authorities and are ultimately responsible for the decisions that affect the children and the family. When parents are attentive to their own feelings, the wisdom of the five messengers can provide guidance for the tough and rewarding job of raising children.

Trauma

By their very nature, traumatic events stimulate overwhelming emotional experiences that require unusual, often extraordinary, coping strategies. Our responses to trauma are in many ways a testament to the human spirit and sometimes underscore humankind's creative capacity for survival. Victims of serious accidents, natural disasters, war, crime, or abuse are often traumatized by these experiences, but any event that is experienced as extremely threatening and stimulates an overwhelming sense of fear could be called traumatic.

Immediate reactions to traumatic events typically involve primitive survival instincts, but these can be quite varied. Depending upon the individual and the nature and extent of the trauma, symptoms may include confusion, detachment, blunted affect, hyper-arousal, agitation, or dissociation. In response to the immediate crisis, these symptoms can serve a life-preserving function, helping the traumatized person distance him- or herself from further danger or maintain a detached emotional demeanor that prevents panic or irrational behavior that might lead to further risk. Once the threat of the traumatic event has passed, survivors of the trauma may experience post-traumatic symptoms including, among others, extreme anxiety, social withdrawal, intrusive thoughts or memories of the traumatic event, sleep disturbance, avoidant behaviors, or flashbacks—intense recollections of the event that may be triggered by reminders of the trauma.

In the aftermath of a traumatic event, crisis counseling or critical incident debriefing can help victims by providing them with a framework for understanding their often-troubling symptoms and by getting victims in touch with resources for additional help as needed. The need for psychological assistance following a traumatic event is becoming well known and more acceptable, and many organizations routinely provide this help when the need arises. Once the crisis has passed, many individuals enter a phase known as pseudo-adjustment, in which there is a period of relative calm and normalcy based around the notion that the end of the traumatic event means the end of emotional difficulties related to the incident. When the post-traumatic symptoms mentioned above become increasingly unmanageable, or when alcohol, obsessive work, or other efforts to control the symptoms become a problem, some people turn to psychotherapy for help.

Normal daily functioning requires some sense of control over our environment; we journey through our days secure in the belief that we have the power to keep ourselves safe and to influence the course of our daily lives. When trauma strikes, our sense of control is severely challenged and sometimes completely shattered. Our lives and our destiny are dictated by the trauma, and our self-protective responses are often automatic. There is no room for reflection or thoughtful consideration of options; fear is the overwhelming emotion, and the choices it inspires occur without conscious thought.

Survivors of traumatic events often refer to their reactions at the time of the crisis as a sense of operating on "automatic pilot" until they were clear of the danger. This experience of detachment from the emotional experience is known as dissociation, and it can be of critical value in helping victims get through a traumatic event as efficiently as possible, without overt emotional expression which might interfere with the immediate task of survival. Many people have heroic fantasies about how they would respond to an encounter with an armed robber, but when this rare event actually happens, almost everyone responds exactly the same way. The overwhelming experience of fear directs the victim's behavior toward self-preservation, which typically involves responding to the attacker with nonconfrontational deference, compliance, and cooperation. Automatic life-preserving reactions such as these are the norm when people encounter sudden, overwhelming threats to their safety.

Only after the threat is gone are people free to experience the full range of their emotional reactions, which involves most, if not all, of the five messengers. When the self-protective strategies employed to deal with the crisis are no longer needed, and when the period of pseudo-adjustment passes, emotions are free to surface. The appearance of the vigilant triad—anger, sadness, and fear—is typically unexpected and often intrudes upon one's life by showing up in irrational or disruptive forms in home, work, and social settings.

When clients enter therapy to address these concerns, one of the goals of treatment is to help them reestablish a healthy, balanced relationship with their feelings. Once clients know the therapy setting is safe, they are free to set aside the self-protective detachment and can begin to look at the full range of emotions surrounding the traumatic event. Anger, sadness, and fear are always part of the emotional response to trauma, and the therapist's role usually involves helping the client validate these emotions as normal and important. Feelings sometimes present as complex combinations of two or more of the five messengers, such as shame or survivor guilt, and require special attention before their wisdom can be appreciated. Ultimately, healing is a process of empowerment in which the survivor of a traumatic event reclaims ownership of the feelings involved and uses the guidance of the messengers to make healthy, emotionally informed choices.

In some ways, survivors of traumatic events are forever marked by their experiences in that they know something about life that most people are blissfully ignorant of. Attention to the messengers offers survivors of traumatic events valuable guidance long after a sense of balance has been restored. Many survivors express a need to apply their unique knowledge in some meaningful way and have volunteered or sought careers in victim assistance programs, rape crisis centers, disaster relief work, or other efforts that offer support to traumatized people. Other survivors offer their assistance more informally when they hear of someone who is having an experience similar to their own. Still others are not interested in offering assistance per se, but they may incorporate their own experiences into a commitment to living life more fully and authentically.

Just as there is no right or wrong way to go through the process of healing, there is no right or wrong way to apply one's experience to life after trauma. Attention to a survivor's own feelings will ultimately offer the guidance needed for making satisfying choices for the future.

The impact of trauma is even more complicated when the traumatic event is of a longstanding nature and is repeated over time. It is a sad fact that child abuse affects millions of children, and the impact of this mistreatment has far-reaching implications for the individual and for society. Children who experience emotional, physical, and/or sexual abuse as a recurring reality of childhood are usually unable to access help from the world at large and must rely upon internal resources to cope with the impact of the abuse. With few or no other options available, children often rely upon the mind's innate capacity to detach from overwhelming pain and find relative safety in dissociation.

Dissociation is often seen in adults who experience accidents, criminal attacks, combat, or other traumatic events; it is a temporary state that helps the person survive the trauma. When children must rely upon dissociation to get through repeated traumatic abuse, emotional detachment can become a way of life. These children develop role-appropriate behavior for different settings that requires them to put the emotional pain of the abuse aside while attending to the demands of school and social life. These dramatically different roles exist independently of one another as children learn to live by a strategy of dissociation. Instead of the relatively fluid emotional states typically seen in childhood, children who have a private life of abuse often develop rigid boundaries between emotions, usually keeping their feelings surrounding their traumatic life hidden from others and from themselves.

When children who employ dissociative survival strategies grow into adulthood, the compartmentalized emotions often persist long after they have gotten away from the source of their childhood trauma. Even though dissociation is no longer necessary for survival, the history of detachment from strong emotions may evolve into a dissociative approach to dealing with feelings. When this coping strategy is no longer needed, its effectiveness often begins to break down, and adult survivors of childhood abuse may start to experience emotional difficulties that compel them to seek professional help. Irrational expressions of anger, sadness, or fear, intrusive thoughts or memories, unexplained problems with sex, or parenting issues are a few of the concerns that surface as individuals begin to address the impact of their own abusive childhoods.

The healing process involves transforming the tendency to automatically detach from strong and challenging emotions into a normal emotional experience. This transformation requires clients to use the safety of the therapy setting to talk about the traumatic events and to begin to acknowledge and accept the associated emotions. While terrible stories of childhood abuse may surface in the course of treatment, the focus of treatment is not on the stories themselves but on the establishment of a normal relationship with feelings. When clients learn that all emotions can be experienced and expressed safely, the need for a dissociative approach fades away, and the feelings can be seen not as things to be avoided but as welcome messengers and guides.

Sometimes the boundaries that have been established between emotional states are very strong, and some adult survivors of childhood traumatic abuse relate to the world and to themselves with extreme fragmentation of role functioning. This fragmented approach is the basis of dissociative identity disorder, or DID, and individuals who carry this diagnosis experience themselves as having distinct parts of their personality that operate independently of one another. Formerly known as multiple personality disorder, this condition is not the bizarre illness represented in soap operas and cheesy crime dramas; rather, it is a primitive defense, typically constructed in early childhood, which attempts to protect the person from being emotionally overwhelmed. I use the word *primitive* because it is a very basic and somewhat simplistic effort to deny or detach from strong, feared emotions.

It is notable that virtually all people who are diagnosed with DID have distinct parts of their identity that represent the different messengers: there is always a part that experiences anger, another part that experiences happiness, and so on. The treatment of DID is no different from the approach to treating other post-trauma disorders. The establishment of a safe and secure therapy setting allows for the acknowledgment of emotions related to the trauma and eventually leads to acceptance of the feelings as valid responses to overwhelming distress. This acceptance leads to personal empowerment and allows the five messengers to offer guidance that can be attended to. The fluid movement of the messengers in response to the environment is important but cannot occur when there are rigid boundaries between the messengers and that environment. When DID clients learn they no longer need to protect themselves by relying upon the boundaries to detach from feelings, the boundaries fade away, revealing a natural state of integration.

ALL ROADS LEAD TO HOME

I hope that I have not oversimplified things by providing only a thumbnail sketch of each of the clinical diagnoses and issues discussed in this chapter. My intention has been to show that while their presentations may vary, the messengers are intimately involved in all clinical issues. Books have been written about these clinical topics, and many therapists participate in postgraduate training in order to offer specialized services for particular clinical populations. While aspects of treatment are unique to each clinical condition, all treatment approaches are ultimately different roads to the same destination. Regardless of the issue that brings someone to therapy, recovery or healing is a subjective experience involving the client's sense of internal balance or peace of mind. A clear and healthy relationship with the five messengers offers clients a vehicle for self-evaluation where peace and balance are concerned.

Even individuals of diminished mental capacity, such as those who suffer from mental retardation, or those who suffer from a major biochemically based mental condition, such as schizophrenia, face the challenge of learning how to use the guidance of their feelings to make the choices that are in their best interest. Therapists who work with these challenging individuals recognize that self-care and ongoing self-management require clients, to the extent that they are able, to learn to respond to their feelings in effective and appropriate ways.

Whether one is working through a clinical condition or working to live a more authentic and satisfying life, one crucial element is required: courage. The desire to change does not come easily; people are usually more comfortable with that which is familiar, and challenging the standard way of doing things always involves uncertainty and risk. *Encouragement* is the act of enabling courage in another person, and it is an important part of any friendship or parenting relationship. Encouragement is part of the therapy process as well, and clients often show great courage in taking on the difficult challenge of facing their problems and their pain. The courage that inspires people to work toward a better relationship with their own feelings is always rewarded with a greater sense of balance and peace of mind.

HARMONY AND DISSONANCE
THE DANCE OF MIXED EMOTIONS

Harmony allows for occasional dissonance, but overall, the melody prevails.
—Emilia E. Martinez-Brawley

This entire book focuses on an exploration of the five essential emotions, so it may seem odd when I say that anger, sadness, fear, happiness, and love are not feelings at all. These distinct emotional categories are merely the names we use to communicate about internal experiences, but the feelings themselves are personal, subjective emotional events. No discussion of feelings can take place without these labels, but since the messengers are ultimately experiences, not words, any attempt to assign them to discreet categories is somewhat arbitrary.

Nonetheless, I have used these labels to try to present what appear to be the five universally experienced emotional states, and I trust I have done so in a way that recognizes and allows for the uniqueness of each individually experienced feeling. Discussion can become much more difficult, however, when an emotional event involves two or more feelings presenting in close proximity to one another.

As I write this, I am looking at a chart in a book on human relations training that lists 217 words that describe feelings. Similar charts and tables have been developed for working with children to help them learn a vocabulary for communicating about their emotions. One might ask, "If there are hundreds of words that describe different feelings, how is it possible to distill all feelings down to five messengers?" It is a good and fair question, but it can be easily answered when we consider the concepts of *degree* and *combination.*

The spectrum of emotional intensity has been discussed in each of the chapters devoted to a particular messenger, as has the notion that each feeling presents along a continuum ranging from very mild to very intense. Many different words describe the varying degrees of any one emotion. For example, on the list of 217 feeling words, 17 of them describe varying degrees of fear. Those 17 include nervous, apprehensive, unsure, and terrified—in addition to 13 others—but each word represents a different point on the continuum of fear. The variety of emotional vocabulary adds linguistic spice to our discussions about feelings, but there is no universal standard for consensus about what a particular feeling word feels like. Most people would see an obvious difference between feeling *unsure* and feeling *terrified,* but who can say whether a person who feels *tense* is more or less uncomfortable than someone who feels *nervous?* In the end, everyone must come to terms with his or her own personal vocabulary for describing the variations of emotional experience. Living an authentic and balanced life requires us to attend to the wisdom and guidance of the messengers wherever they appear on the emotional spectrum.

Appreciating the varying degrees of an emotion is difficult at times and can become even more so when feelings manifest in concert with one another. When people talk about situations that involve mixed emotions, they often have difficulty articulating what they feel. When asked directly, "How do you feel about that?" many people will respond with opinions, hopes, or wishes rather than statements about their feelings. This tendency is often observed in therapy sessions. A client who was asked how she felt about a relative who kept offering unsolicited advice about her marriage told me, "I feel like she should keep her opinions to herself." When I asked a bright high school senior who was showing sudden academic problems how he felt about going to college in a few months, he replied, "It's going to be a whole new world."

While an astute listener might infer feelings from each of these responses, such inferences can only be speculation, since the clients themselves never really answered the question "How do you feel about that?" In both of these cases, the clients had mixed feelings about their given circumstances. The client with the nosey relative was angry about the intrusion and fearful of pushing her family member away by confronting her directly. The student was happy about getting accepted to his chosen college and about the prospect of experiencing some independence, but he was also fearful about the unknown challenges he would be facing and sad about leaving close friendships behind.

Attending to our feelings, understanding their messages, and following their guidance toward satisfying choices may be sound advice, but it is not always easy. When mixed emotions are involved, it is even harder and requires a willingness to appreciate all the feelings involved. A large vocabulary is available with which to identify combinations of feelings, and each of these combinations can usually be broken down into their component parts. Communicating in the vocabulary of mixed emotions is sometimes difficult, however, because of the uncertainty of an agreed-upon mix of feelings. For example, when someone talks about feeling "confused," he or she might be referring to any possible combination of the five messengers. A new mother might be confused by her mixed feelings of love and fear, while a grieving widow might call the mix of anger and sadness confusion. Acknowledging the confusion is important, but understanding it and benefiting from it require looking at the emotional ingredients that make up the mixed emotional experience.

AN INVITATION TO THE DANCE

When someone follows a recipe for baking a chocolate cake, that person can be reasonably certain the cake will taste the same each time it is prepared. The recipe calls for prescribed amounts of specific ingredients, and the finished product will always be recognized as a chocolate cake, never a cheesecake. If mixed emotional states were made this way, everyone would know the exact proportions of feelings involved any time a word was used to describe an emotional experience. When someone expressed frustration, everyone would know that the person was referring to an emotional experience that is 61 percent anger, 7 percent sadness, and 32 percent fear. The person would still have to face the personal challenge of attending to each of the emotional components, but everyone would understand what the person was experiencing, and the individual could consult his or her recipe book to determine how much time to allocate to each of the messengers.

I present this somewhat absurd notion to show that there is no cookbook for mixed emotions. Whether they present in pure or mixed form, all feelings are subjective, and the words we use to describe a mixed emotional state reflect a personal combination of experiential elements, not a specific formula.

Regarding mixed emotions, an appreciation of the value of the messengers requires allowing for the presentation of all the component parts, although this task presents several challenges. First, it is impossible to attend to each and every emotional part at the same time. Second, mixed emotional states sometimes involve conflicting feelings, which may be experienced as incompatible or mutually exclusive. Third, any attempt to logically sort and order the component feelings may encounter resistance from the messengers themselves, who may have their own sense of priority and urgency. In fact, it is this third point that offers the best opportunity for awareness of the various messengers involved in any mixed emotion.

When we accept the mixed emotional state as a combination of two or more essential messengers, we can begin to ask ourselves, "What am I feeling?" If we take the time necessary to listen for an answer, the various messengers will present themselves in a natural process that can be likened to a dance. An elemental part of the mixed feelings will move forward into awareness for a time and then recede as another aspect of the mix moves forward into awareness. It is sometimes a slow dance in which one emotion lingers before allowing another emotion to take its place. At other times it is almost frenetic in tempo as one of the emotional components moves to the front of awareness briefly, only to be rapidly replaced by another feeling. Regardless of the cadence, when they are allowed to present themselves, the messengers that make up a mixed emotional state will move into consciousness in a manner that allows us to consider what they are trying to tell us about a given experience.

If we are not open to seeing the various messengers involved in a mixed emotional state, then we block our own pathway and prevent the opportunity to learn from their wisdom. All that is necessary in order for us to begin the process that will allow us to be aware of the messengers is a willingness to consider the different feelings involved in mixed or conflicting emotions. Settling down long enough to become aware of the feelings involved can be challenging, especially with feelings that are at the strong end of the intensity continuum, but it is the only way to welcome the messengers with some level of clarity. Some suggestions for cultivating and honing this ability will be offered in the next chapter, but I can state here that curiosity, interest, and practice are important factors.

A TALE OF TWO FEELINGS

Any mixed emotion can provide someone with an opportunity to practice attending to the component messengers. Not long ago I found myself home alone on a rainy Saturday afternoon with nothing to do. My wife had been given two great tickets to a Washington Wizards basketball game, and she and my son were at the arena. I had no pressing chores or obligations and nothing begging for my attention. I tried to see what my friends were up to but couldn't reach anyone. I had already been to the gym that morning, and I didn't feel like reading. You would think that I would have cherished this rare opportunity to relax, but when I tired of channel surfing and raiding the refrigerator, I had to face the truth: I was bored.

Once I acknowledged my boredom I decided to apply what I have been writing about to my own situation. I relaxed, became curious about what I was feeling, and allowed the messengers to present themselves. The first feeling I became aware of was anger, and when I paid attention, it became clear to me that things felt pretty unfair. My sense of injustice would have been written with a lowercase eye, but my personal list of perceived injustices included the rain, the unavailability of friends, the lack of a third ticket to the Wizards game, and the dearth of anything interesting on TV.

I sat with the feeling until it receded and was replaced with sadness. My perceived losses included the temporary loss of social connections, engaging activities, and opportunities for fun. I sat a little while longer until the messengers invited the question, "What do you want to do about this?" Then I made some choices: I changed the strings on my guitar and worked on some songs. I called my sister in New York and spoke with her for a while. When my wife and son returned home, I was sitting in front of my laptop, working on this book.

From a certain perspective, my reflective response to everyday boredom might seem overly analytical and self-indulgent, and it would be easy to say, "If you're bored, just get up and do something!" Ultimately, that is exactly what I did, but by taking the short time needed to pay attention to what was a very ordinary emotional experience, my choices were informed and personally satisfying. I could have busied myself with some activity to avoid the mixed emotions of boredom, but the feelings of anger and sadness would likely have asserted themselves in some fashion down the road. Maybe they would have been expressed by my moping around the house all day in some mildly annoyed state, or perhaps they would have shown up in some passive-aggressive behavior toward my wife and son when they came home. Instead, I actually enjoyed the choices I made to respond to the boredom, and I was able to get some vicarious enjoyment from my family's excitement about the NBA game they had seen. All in all, I consider it a pretty good return for an investment of a few minutes of reflection.

Now let me present another scenario involving the same two emotions. A high school junior came to see me to address intense feelings of jealousy surrounding her ex-boyfriend's relationship with another girl. Her jealousy had become a near obsession, and she found herself going to extreme lengths to find out what they were doing, where they were going, and how serious the new relationship had become. To her credit, the young woman realized that her focus had become unhealthy, and she wanted to try to restore a sense of normalcy to her life.

With encouragement and the supportive inquiry of therapy, she started to do something she had not done before: she became curious about the jealousy and allowed herself to begin to appreciate its emotional components. First came sadness, inviting her to acknowledge the sense of loss that followed the sudden breakup of her eight-month-long relationship. The losses included the perceived loss of friendship, closeness, and affection that she had experienced with the boyfriend. Then came anger, inviting her to consider the sense of injustice she was experiencing, which included the unfairness of the boyfriend breaking up with her suddenly, by email, a few days before Valentine's Day, and the perceived unfairness of him quickly starting to date the new girlfriend.

Sometimes what people experience as jealousy also includes feelings of fear, but that was not what appeared to my client as

HARMONY and DISSONANCE

she listened to her own emotions. Her feelings appeared to her in an alternating flow of sadness and anger, and she became aware of various personal truths as she continued to attend to the feelings. She was sad about the loss of a romantic relationship and about the loss of other friendships that had faded with her singular interest in the boyfriend. She was angry with the new girlfriend for taking her place in the boy's affections and angry about the unfairness of not having a date for the prom.

Eventually, she came to see her obsessive behavior as an unhealthy effort to gain control over her sense of loss and injustice. Acceptance of the feelings did not bring the boyfriend back, nor did it eliminate all of the pain around the breakup. Attending to the messengers merely paved the way for her to make healthier choices, which included renewing her interest in gymnastics, reconnecting with friends, focusing on schoolwork, and trying to enjoy the remainder of her high school experience.

Anger and sadness were essential elements in both my boredom and my client's jealousy, though everyone would agree that boredom and jealousy are not the same emotional experience. The difference can be attributed to individual emotional alchemy: that is, differing subjective experiences of the combination and intensity of the feelings. The identified mixed emotional states—boredom and jealousy—are the names that we assigned to our personal experiences of the combined feelings. As boredom or jealousy, they are words that identify personal experiences, but they have limited value in communicating feelings to other people, and their value as messengers and guides is obscured by the mixed nature of the messengers involved.

The feelings that compose a mixed emotion may be conflicting or complementary, but when they remain mixed they are often confusing and can be difficult to appreciate and understand. When we take the time to acknowledge and value the various feelings involved in any mixed emotion, however, it is easier to share our experience with others. Moreover, when they are allowed to present themselves as individual elements of a mixed emotional state, the messengers can be attended to and are free to offer their wisdom and guidance. Mixed emotions may be one of the rare circumstances in which the whole is actually less than the sum of its parts.

IN THE MIXING BOWL

Consider these few examples of the names we give to various combinations of emotions.

Vigilant Triad Mixes—Mixed emotional states involving some combination of anger, sadness, and fear include envy, uncertainty, resentment, helplessness, disgust, and disappointment.

Desired Duo Mixes—When happiness and love are both present, the mixed emotional states include affection, passion, fondness, infatuation, tenderness, relief, and enchantment.

Triad-Duo Mixes—The feelings of the vigilant triad and those of the desired duo are not mutually exclusive. Some examples of mixed emotional states containing some combination of triad feelings and duo feelings include concern, compassion, sympathy, empathy, bravery, determination, and adventurousness.

These selected examples are arbitrary, and they represent only a very cursory listing of the names given to various mixed emotions. When we consider that mixed emotional states can be made up of any combination of feelings, and that the feelings can come from any point on the spectrum of intensity, the number of possible mixes is astronomical. Sometimes such words as *overwhelmed, frustrated,* or *confused* are as close as we can come to naming an unfamiliar state of mixed emotions.

Experience, education, and culture are just a few of the factors that contribute to the development of an individual's personal vocabulary for identifying mixed emotional states. For example, one person might consider *lethargic* to be the perfect word to describe a particular set of feelings, while the same word may have no personal meaning to someone else. Idiomatic words or phrases, like *stoked, wiggin',* or *off the hook,* often have emotionally descriptive meaning within a specific subculture or age group, but they may not be part of mainstream vocabulary.

The language we use to identify the wide range of mixed emotions can be called our personal poetry. These words are used to describe the internal emotional landscape and, like all poetry, they often evoke emotional associations in the people we are communicating with. They are potentially powerful elements of our language and can be used to draw people to us or to push people away. Words that identify mixed emotions are a tribute to our desire to express and communicate the complex and intricate workings of our emotional nature.

Although mixed emotions are made up of some combination of the five feelings, the language we use to identify and express emotional states does not in itself give us access to each component messenger. Sometimes expression is all that is desired, but when we want to use a moment of mixed emotion for guidance, we must let the mixture settle and separate, revealing the messengers in the mix. When we allow ourselves the opportunity to attend to all the messengers involved in a mixed emotional state, we can benefit from the guidance of their collective wisdom.

9.

PRACTICE

Practice, which some regard as a chore, should be approached as just about the most pleasant recreation ever devised.

—Babe Didrickson Zaharias

Some activities are difficult to practice simply because they are expensive or they require special equipment or a special location. In this regard, cultivating a relationship with the five messengers is more like running than skiing or swimming because practice can take place pretty much anytime and anywhere. No matter how convenient it is, however, no one can be forced to practice against his or her will.

I hope this book has stimulated interest in the five messengers and the reader has come to appreciate that a healthy relationship with one's own feelings provides an internal compass for making the best choices available. Building and maintaining that healthy relationship requires a commitment to remaining mindful of the messengers, a commitment that can be pleasantly strengthened through practice. Practicing anything requires effort, and the practice involved in learning about our feelings can take us outside our comfort zones.

Many people seek refuge in the comfort of what is known rather than risking the discomfort of that which is unknown, but what they refer to as comfort is sometimes just familiarity. When we rely on familiarity to avoid spending time with our feelings, we are destined, or doomed, to the same old programmed responses to the call of our emotions. Fortunately, as the quotation at the start of this chapter suggests, practice need not be a chore. In fact, the discipline of developing and sustaining a good relationship with one's feelings can become a valued and pleasant part of everyday life.

In the following sections I offer some suggestions for specific ways to cultivate a relationship with the messengers, but I want to emphasize that these activities are merely suggestions and that the opportunity to practice attending to the messengers is always with us. Any time we pause and take a moment to reflect upon what we are feeling, we are strengthening our relationship with one or more messengers through *in situ* practice. Practicing in real-life situations is perhaps the best way to cultivate a relationship with feelings because the messages and guidance that follow sincere reflection reinforce the value of the practice.

Whether practice is spontaneous or planned, one thing is required for the practice to be of benefit: the conscious intention of making contact with feelings. Approaching practice as a chance to learn about feelings does not guarantee that the messages will be comfortable or easy, but they will be personal and authentic. A former client whose need to control emotions eventually yielded to a more honest acceptance of his feelings once told me, "I have finally learned to stop clinging to false certainty and have started embracing true uncertainty."

EXPERIENCE AND REFLECTION

Our experience of the world is revealed to us through the wisdom of the five messengers, but that experience arrives through the portal of one or more of the five senses. We see, hear, touch, taste, or smell something before the rapid sequence of events begins that sends signals to our brains, stimulates our feelings, and sounds a call to action. If we approach the five feelings—anger, sadness, fear, happiness, and love—with mindfulness and the intention of learning more about ourselves, any sensory experience can open the door to self-discovery.

The process of learning from the messengers has two parts, however: experience and reflection. Experience comprises the physical and biochemical components of an emotional state; reflection is the process that allows us to assign personal meaning to the experience and to apply our emotional experience to the choices we make. Appreciating and benefiting from the wisdom of the five messengers requires experience and reflection to work together for the common good, and both our experiential and our reflective abilities can be enhanced through practice.

THE SENSORY GATEWAY

Without emotion there is nothing to reflect upon, so I will first offer some suggestions for intentionally stimulating emotional experience. As stated earlier, any experience, from reading a newspaper to making love, evokes feelings, and any feeling presents an opportunity for learning. The following ideas are offered in the spirit of encouraging the reader's own curiosity about what he or she can do to intentionally stimulate feelings as part of the process of cultivating a satisfying relationship with the five messengers. Since all emotion begins with sensation, these ideas focus on ordinary sensory experiences as a gateway to the world of feelings.

The Visual Arts

Any visual experience can stimulate feelings, but the world of visual art offers countless images created specifically to evoke emotions. Paintings, drawings, sculptures, photographs, and other visual media reflect the emotional experience of the artist who created them, though there is no way of knowing whether the experience of the person viewing the artwork bears any resemblance to the artist's own experience. This is one of the truly intriguing aspects of all works of art, which ultimately renders the artist's intention irrelevant.

When you take in a work of visual art, simply allow the emotional experience to reveal itself. An analytic approach to a piece of artwork may be fine for an art history classroom, but the emotional experience is what you are after in building a relationship with the messengers.

Do not limit yourself to familiar or comfortable styles or themes. The emotions evoked by art that you would not hang in your home are just as relevant as the feelings stimulated by a cherished masterpiece. Emotionally evocative visual art can be created by experienced artists or by amateurs and can be found in the most famous art museums as well as in the hallways of elementary schools. I have personally been deeply moved both by the Statue of Liberty and by a collection of family snapshots in the United States Holocaust Memorial Museum, though the emotional experiences were vastly different. When you look for opportunities to use the visual arts to further your awareness of feelings, you will find the world to be a gallery of unlimited potential.

Music

Listening to live or recorded music is a wonderful way to stimulate emotional experience. As with any art form, tastes vary widely: the soulful aria an opera lover enjoys may sound like nails scraping across a chalkboard to a country western fan, but exposing yourself to different forms of music provides an opportunity to experience a broad range of emotions. Music is a central feature of many cultures, and the unique quality of different musical forms can give rise to subtle variations of feelings you have never experienced previously.

Music has been employed in celebrations ranging from weddings to funerals, and it is often created with the intention of evoking a particular emotional state, as in the case of movie soundtracks or religious choral works. The composer's or the performer's intent, however, is unimportant in any effort to learn about your own feelings. All you need to do is expose yourself to music and allow your own emotional experience to speak for itself.

When you approach music with the intention of experiencing the messengers, even incidental music, such as radio jingles or elevator music, can offer emotional access through the auditory gateway. High-quality live or recorded music, however, has an extraordinary power to evoke emotions. I was recently browsing in a local specialty shop that carries only one or two brands of high-end stereo equipment I could never afford. I struck up a wonderful conversation with the storeowner about the difference between average and high-quality stereo systems. He led me to a private listening room where he featured his top-of-the-line system, and he played one of my favorite cuts from a Rickie Lee Jones CD. The previously unheard nuances of her voice and the accompaniment washed over me, stirring up a dance of emotions that is difficult to describe.

"How's that feel?" he asked.

I didn't know how to answer him. "It's amazing," I said. "I don't know how to put it into words."

The shop owner smiled proudly and pronounced, "*That's* my mission statement."

Performing Arts

Stories or impressionistic images created through the performing arts can be emotionally evocative experiences and can arouse the full range of feelings. Theater, film, TV, and dance performances often have this capacity, but any performance—even a street juggler or a circus act—offers stimulation that invites the presence of the messengers. From light comedies to intense dramas, from tap dance to ballet, the quality of a performance is usually judged by the emotional impression it makes upon the audience member.

Performing arts are deeply rooted in human cultures and can be traced to primitive celebrations of important events. In prehistoric times, plays and dances that re-created and celebrated nature, hunting, birth, and death were vehicles for communicating and sharing the emotional experience of these events with the individual's tribe or group. Civilization has grown and developed over the centuries, but the performing arts continue to recognize, celebrate, and draw our attention to the shared experience of the things that make us angry, sad, fearful, happy, or loving.

If your intention is to learn more about your messengers, experience different kinds of performing arts; even attend a performance that may expose you to feelings you do not ordinarily seek out. In making your choices, do not be too narrow in your scope; strong emotional experiences can sometimes be found in unexpected performances. Along with all the other messengers, I have experienced sadness during theatrical performances many times, but no performance has ever made me as sad as some of the episodes of *Lassie* I watched when I was a child.

Reading

If you have any doubt about the emotionally evocative power of reading, simply ask a child to describe the characters and plot twists in the *Harry Potter* books. The written word can span the range of feelings within a few pages; it can take readers to emotional experiences of images and ideas that play out in the privacy of their own mind. From comic books to newspapers to classics, any form of writing has this potential, and the virtually unlimited amount of reading material available allows us to abandon unsatisfying and emotionally uninspired works in favor of something more stimulating.

If, on the one hand, your desire is to explore the experience of a particular messenger, it is easy to choose a book to evoke that particular feeling. On the other hand, learning about the messengers can simply be a by-product of reading for study or pleasure, and the feelings can arise in response to wherever the words take you. A "good" read is ultimately measured by the relationship with feelings that it inspires in the reader.

A lot of writing is intended as a presentation of facts, and emotional responses are of secondary concern to the writer. Poetry, however, is aimed directly at the reader's or the listener's emotions. When I was a small child, my mother would read to me from Robert Louis Stevenson's *A Child's Garden of Verses.* The feelings associated with images of sailing through the sky, digging holes in the sand, and living in the confusing world of grown-ups remain sweet memories to this day. My experience in school, however, virtually sucked all of the life out of poetry. Poems became something to analyze and figure out; what the poet "meant" became more important than how the poem felt.

I was fortunate enough to have a great poetry teacher in college, and I was reintroduced to the emotional experience of poetry. Poetry therapist Peggy Heller illustrates the emotional power of words when she asks students to consider the difference among these three popular sayings: "Gather ye rosebuds while ye may"; "A stitch in time saves nine"; and "Strike while the iron is hot." The "do it now" message may be the same in all three sayings, but the emotional meaning is clearly different. In using poetry to stimulate the presence of the messengers, read many different poets, read poetry aloud, and attend live poetry readings. Don't spend much time trying to figure out the meaning of a poem; where poetry is concerned, the messenger is the message.

Physical Activity

To allow the messengers to reach us through the portal of touch, we must engage in physical contact with the world. Whether the physical activity is gentle and soothing or vigorous and exhausting, emotions are often part of the experience, and attending to the feelings associated with different tactile experiences is an easy way to spend time with one or more of the messengers. You can make a conscious effort to engage in new and different physical experiences to invite intense emotion; helicopter bungee jumping will undoubtedly expose you to new dimensions of fear. Or you can simply pay attention to the feelings involved in touching everyday objects and engaging in the physical activity of ordinary life. A sculptor friend of mine used to pick up a different stone each morning and handle it at various times throughout the day just because he liked the feelings that the different surfaces evoked.

As with all sensual experiences, personal associations play a role in our making emotional connections. The feelings associated with climbing a ladder are different for a professional firefighter from what they are for someone who is afraid of heights. But all emotions are ultimately personal in nature, and attention to the feelings that accompany physical experiences—from washing dishes to hugging—can help you in your effort to develop a relationship with your messengers.

Organized physical activities, such as exercise, yoga, sports, dancing, or adventure outings with clubs, offer opportunities to develop awareness of personal emotional experience in a supportive and guided setting. Participating in organized or pick-up sports adds the dimension of competition, which has its own emotional realities, but it can offer a level of intensity that may enhance the physical or emotional experience. To borrow the tagline of *ABC's Wide World of Sports,* participation in competitive sports offers the opportunity to experience "the thrill of victory and the agony of defeat."

Taste and Smell

Like the other senses, taste and smell have the ability to stir up emotions, often in a very direct and primitive way. You can experience a variety of feelings simply by exposing yourself to different food and drink and paying attention to the emotions they evoke. The sense of taste also evokes familiar emotional associations. Some foods remind us in a visceral way of feelings we associate with our childhood. For many people, Christmas would not be the same without the taste of homemade sugar cookies. For other people, the feelings associated with being forced to eat vegetables as a child compel them to avoid broccoli at all costs.

Emotional associations with certain smells are also uniquely personal. The smell of cow manure undoubtedly stimulates feelings for a gardener or a cowboy that are quite different from the feelings it stimulates for someone with an urban lifestyle. Exposing yourself to different smells in nature, or to manufactured fragrances, can give rise to both subtle and profound emotions. A salesperson once helped enlighten me to the world of perfume by referring to the various fragrances as "music for the nose."

Nature

For active participants and casual observers alike, the natural world offers countless opportunities to stimulate emotional experiences. The messengers themselves are the very essence of human nature, and the survival of the species is a testament to the relationship between our emotions and the world around us. A simple walk in the woods allows all the senses to engage with nature and invites an array of emotional responses. For that matter, if we are attentive to them, our feelings will be immediately apparent while we dig in a garden or watch a lightning storm.

If the world of nature is your chosen vehicle for learning more about the messengers, consider stretching your comfort zone to include all the elements. A white-water rafting trip is no better or no worse than watching birds fight over a piece of bread in a park, but the two activities are likely to give rise to different emotions. Feelings associated with cold-weather activities may be quite different from those associated with lying on a beach in the sunshine. As with all sensory engagements, emotional associations and experiences vary widely. A child's emotional experience of a midweek snowstorm, for example, is usually quite different from an adult's experience of it.

Pursuing Your Passion

In the previous sections I suggested some ways to evoke emotional experience through active engagement of the five senses. The suggestions I have offered represent a small fraction of the possibilities for inviting the presence of the messengers, and they are intended as a vehicle for stimulating the reader's own creative efforts in pursuit of emotional experience. I emphasized the value of the arts and nature toward this end, but as stated earlier, any sensory experience can point the way to feelings. The uniquely personal nature of all emotional experience is a recurring theme in this book, and everyone must make personal choices in his or her efforts to practice emotional awareness.

If you are uncertain which path is right for you, consider pursuing your passions. Most people have hobbies, activities, or interests they are passionate about, though sometimes the demands of everyday life conspire to cause them to abandon interests that were once fulfilling. In an effort to connect with your feelings, consider digging out your Rollerblades or musical instrument or scrapbook. Revisit projects you set aside, or pursue an activity you have always wanted to try. Community groups, schools, and recreation centers typically offer classes and activities that cater to a wide range of interests and accommodate people's work schedules.

Curiosity is all you need to pursue an interest that could provide ongoing opportunities for varied emotional experiences. Of course, curiosity will not always lead to something that inspires passion, but it will always stimulate feelings. A client of mine recently explored a hobby she had long been curious about by enrolling in a sailing course. She completed the course, only to discover that sailing was not what she had hoped it would be. She had satisfied her curiosity, nevertheless, and moved on to pursuing other interests.

When we are engaged in interests and activities we feel passionate about, we offer an open invitation to all the messengers. Joy and frustration are part of any passion, be it stamp collecting or surfing, and the chance to experience different emotions is always present. Simply exploring opportunities to learn more about the things that intrigue you will eventually lead you to your passions. Perhaps this is just another way of saying that if you listen to your feelings for guidance, they will tell you where to go to practice.

CULTIVATING REFLECTION

When we engage in interests and activities with the intention of tuning in to the accompanying feelings, we will certainly become more aware of the presence of emotions in all aspects of our lives. Being able to identify feelings when they arise, however, is only the first step in the process of building a satisfying relationship with our feelings. In order to appreciate their value as messengers and guides, we must attend to the emotional realities our feelings invite us to consider, and we must apply what we learn to the choices we make. A healthy relationship with one's own messengers provides the guidance necessary for each person to live as peacefully as possible with the consequences of his or her choices. For those who wish to develop and maintain that healthy relationship, personal reflection is necessary.

Reflection involves the willingness to experience, observe, question, and think about feelings and the vital roles they play in our approach to life. As I am using the word, reflection is synonymous with contemplation, or any other word that implies *mindful* consideration. Where feelings are concerned, reflection involves asking oneself some simple questions and listening for the answers. The questions include:

- What am I feeling?
- Is this feeling familiar, and what do I know about it?
- What message does this feeling usually convey, and how does it connect to what I am experiencing in the present?
- What are my options for expressing the feeling?
- Does the feeling invite any other action?
- What choices will I make after spending time with these questions?

I referred to these questions as "simple," and indeed they are, but the process of self-inquiry is often quite difficult. When facing an emotionally challenging situation, most people will rely upon a familiar or habitual response. If the response happens to be consistent with what someone feels, all is well, but if the response is in conflict with someone's true feelings, there will be consequences somewhere down the road. The reflective process takes more conscious effort than does reliance upon familiar responses, but it paves the way to mindful choices that are in harmony with what we feel.

This self-inquisitive process can occur in a matter of seconds, or it can take place over an extended period of time. Sometimes quickly "checking-in" with one's feelings is all that is required to assure a wise and mindful response, whereas some situations need to be mulled over before a satisfying response can be found. Taking the time necessary for reflection will not lead to some universally agreed-upon response, but it will lead the sincere inquisitor to his or her personal truth and will guide the process of making personally satisfying choices.

The reflective process consists of two parts: asking the questions and listening for the answers. Both questioning and listening require sincerity, patience, and commitment—qualities that can be nurtured and strengthened through practice. In this sense, reflection is like any other skill, and practice can make reflection a more comfortable and uncomplicated process. The following activities are offered as potential ways through which you can develop your reflective abilities. As with the suggestions in the preceding sections, these activities are merely a few of the countless possibilities that are available for engaging and strengthening the capacity for exploring the personal meaning of the five messengers. It is my sincere hope that these suggestions stimulate the reader's own creative efforts for developing this most valuable skill.

Take a Walk with Your Feelings

There is simply no way around it. In order to nurture your relationship with the messengers, you have to make a conscious commitment to spending time with your feelings. In theory, this can be done anywhere: if you decide to do it, you can focus on your feelings while sitting at your desk at work or reclining in front of the TV. In reality, however, most people live lives full of distractions, and the likelihood of being interrupted or drawn away from your intended practice is greater when potential distractions are close at hand.

"Taking a walk with your feelings" is both a literal suggestion and a metaphor. Literally, I am suggesting that you leave your cell phone and pager behind and go out and take a walk with the intention of checking in with your emotions. As you stroll, you can begin by asking: "What feeling am I most aware of right now?" or "What have I been feeling lately?" Then, once you become aware of a particular feeling, ask yourself any of the previously suggested questions, and continue walking as you listen for the answers.

Perhaps it would be more accurate to suggest that you listen for a *response* to your question rather than an *answer*. Your mind may respond with specific guidance, or it may take you to thoughts that need to be considered as you deepen your relationship with the messenger. For example, in the process of reflecting upon sadness one might ask, "What do I know about this feeling?" Reflection might conjure up memories of past losses or of images and models of others who have dealt with loss. The response to the question cannot really be called an "answer," but it certainly helps the individual understand and appreciate his or her own personal history with the messenger.

Contemplative walking is simply a vehicle for spending time with your own internal landscape, and it offers the opportunity for undistracted emotional reflection. As a metaphor, "taking a walk with your feelings" simply means making a commitment to putting aside potential interruptions with the intention of inquiring about your own feelings, which can be accomplished with or without moving your feet.

Journaling

Keeping a journal offers an opportunity to practice reflection through the vehicle of the written word. Journaling is a somewhat generic term that can be applied to many forms of personal record keeping, including memoirs, travel experiences, dreams, or favorite recipes. As a tool for developing a relationship with the messengers, keep a feeling journal which focuses on your relationship with your own emotions. The same reflective questions offered earlier can be applied to the process of writing a journal, and the answers and responses that follow the questions will be the same in written or unwritten form. Unlike other forms of reflection, however, journaling offers an opportunity to keep a written record of your process. Old journal entries can serve as points of reference as we develop a relationship with the messengers that will continue throughout our lives.

Some people experience writing as a natural and comfortable activity and are able to express themselves freely through the written word. For others, writing is a chore, and it is certainly not their preferred mode of reflection. If you count yourself among the latter group, I encourage you not to reject the notion of keeping a feeling journal without giving it a try. Often, anxieties about writing are related to unpleasant experiences in school or fears of critique or criticism. One of the nice things about keeping a journal is that you are writing for an audience of one, and you are not required to share your writing with anyone unless you wish to do so. And in personal journal writing, spelling doesn't count! All reflective practice is about the relationship with oneself, and even a reluctant writer may enjoy the freedom this form of reflection offers.

Journaling can be done anytime and virtually anywhere. You can write in your journal when you are focusing on a particular feeling, or you can begin writing with no specific feeling in mind just to see where your sincere inquiry leads you. Occasional and unscheduled journal writing is just fine, but many people find that a commitment to even a few minutes of written emotional reflection on a regular basis helps them maintain and nurture their relationship with the messengers.

Meditation

Meditation is not really a technique for practicing emotional reflection, but it is included in this section because it helps people cultivate a nonreactive mental posture that is critical in any sincere effort to appreciate the messengers. Although meditation, in its many forms, is often associated with Eastern and some Western spiritual practices, I am not promoting any particular philosophy or theology when I discuss it as an adjunct to people's efforts to become emotionally reflective.

Here is a general, nonsectarian way to approach meditation. Find a distraction-free environment where you will be undisturbed for twenty minutes or so. Assume a seated posture that you can comfortably maintain for those twenty minutes. The posture should be erect, but not rigid, and should allow for unrestricted, comfortable breathing. Many meditative disciplines suggest sitting cross-legged on a cushion on the floor, and many practitioners find this to be a comfortable arrangement that supports the proper posture. Nevertheless, if you find this position to be too uncomfortable, sitting in a chair will work just fine. (Lying down or propping your feet up is not recommended.)

Allow your hands to rest comfortably, palms up, in your lap. Allow your eyes to focus on the floor a foot or two in front of you without staring too intently, or close your eyes altogether. Now pay attention to your breathing and mentally count your breaths. Every cycle of inhale and exhale is one count; if this is too difficult, count one the first time you inhale, two the first time you exhale, and so on, up to the number ten. Don't force your breathing; just breathe naturally and count. When you get to ten, start over at one and count to ten again. Just keep doing this until the twenty minutes are up. Practice this discipline every day, twice a day if possible. That's all there is to it.

Sounds easy, doesn't it? Here is what typically happens when people try to meditate for the first time. First, they quickly learn that the twenty-minute daily commitment is more difficult to honor than they thought, and practice becomes a haphazard, catch-as-catch-can thing they abandon in relatively short order. If you choose to stick with it, the first thing you will become aware of is how busy the resting mind is! Getting to ten is not as easy as it sounds, and you will likely find your mind drifting to all kinds of things as you lose track of the breath count. Don't despair; learning to calm the busy mind is the very purpose of meditation. When you realize that you have lost the count, take a centering breath and return to one.

In time, you will be able to spend twenty minutes with a centered and non-distracted mind, but the value of this begins to be seen in an even more generalized way. Meditators usually find they are a little less reactive to the ordinary stress and strain of everyday live. The practice doesn't make people dull, nor does it slow their reaction time, but it appears to help build a sense of mindfulness so that responses to life's demands are more thoughtful and less automatic.

When we apply a mindful and nonreactive approach to our own emotions, we enhance the value of reflective self-inquiry, and meditation can help us develop this capacity. Meditation will not *make* anyone reflect upon his or her feelings, nor will it guarantee that the responses we get from sincere inquiry will be easy to attend to and incorporate. But meditation can help us develop our ability to be mindful with the questions we ask ourselves, and it can help us learn to pause long enough to assure that the responses we get to our own questions are thoughtful and honest.

Personal Growth Retreats

The complexities of life are most meaningful and manageable when attention to the messengers is an integral part of our daily routine. But we all face the challenge of balancing the demands of everyday life with taking time to practice personal check-in and reflection. Attending a retreat is a nice way to set aside time specifically devoted to the practice of emotional reflection and personal growth. In a sense, any "getaway" is a kind of retreat from the familiarity of a predictable schedule. An ordinary vacation offers an opportunity to appreciate life in a different and less stressful setting. A personal growth retreat is essentially a vacation with the specific goal of emotional renewal and development.

A retreat can be a daylong or a weekend experience, or it can span a week or more. Many organizations worldwide offer personal growth retreats, including a number of well-established institutes that publish catalogs offering a variety of retreats centered on particular interests or issues. These institutes routinely sponsor residential workshops on self-care, massage, marriage enrichment, spirituality, midlife crisis, body and movement, and yoga, among many other offerings. Just out of curiosity, I typed the words *personal growth retreats* into Google and received more than 10 million site references!

If you decide to attend a retreat, choose one that appeals to your curiosity or personal interest; any topic will involve an emotional journey, and the messengers are certain to be part of the experience. The retreat leader will offer the structure and guidance necessary to assist you in your efforts, and you will have the opportunity to practice emotional reflection in the company of like-minded others, in a safe and supportive setting.

Choose carefully when selecting a retreat. Get references from your friends and talk to people who have had previous experience with the sponsoring organization and with the retreat leader. Ask whatever questions you need to in order to feel comfortable with your decision. Then take yourself and your messengers on a vacation and become better acquainted.

Psychotherapy

Despite our best efforts at reflection, there are times when we are unable to appreciate and learn from our emotional experiences. When a particular feeling or group of feelings causes us ongoing discomfort, psychotherapy may be helpful. I have never worked with anyone who came to see me because he or she was experiencing too much happiness or love, but virtually every client I have worked with has been struggling with issues related to one or more of the messengers of the vigilant triad. The essential goal of all psychotherapy is to help clients achieve peace of mind, and a healthy relationship with their own feelings is a vital part of the process.

Three major approaches to psychotherapy were discussed in chapter 7, "Finding Balance in the Storm," but there are many other forms of therapy. If you are considering starting therapy, make sure to do your homework first. Read about different approaches to treatment and let your feelings guide you to the approach that makes the most sense to you. Get referrals from your friends or medical professionals, and use the initial session with a psychotherapist to assess whether you feel comfortable with his or her approach. Remember that psychotherapy is a partnership devoted to helping you with your issues and concerns: the therapist is the expert, but you are the consumer, and the therapist works for you. If you choose wisely and make a sincere commitment to the process, psychotherapy is one of the best ways to clear up any debris on the pathway that connects you to your messengers.

A GOOD INVESTMENT

In this chapter I have suggested ways for you to invite emotional experience into your life and for you to cultivate the ability to reflect upon the five feelings when they present themselves. Without experience there is nothing to reflect upon, but without reflection the feelings will never reveal themselves as messengers, and their guidance and wisdom will remain unheard and unheeded. It is my sincere hope that the reader will take my suggestions in the spirit in which they are intended: that is, as encouragement to pursue any opportunity to spend time with feelings and to develop the capacity to consider the messages and the guidance those feelings offer.

There is nothing special about practice. It is merely a conscious effort to develop and maintain a healthy relationship with one's feelings. In a sense, practicing emotional awareness and reflection is also an investment in the future: practice does not "make perfect," but the benefits of practice are realized in the quality of life that accompanies a satisfying relationship with the five messengers.

10.

CONSTANT COMPANIONS

The world is round, and the place which may seem like the end
may also be the beginning.

—Ivy Baker Priest

As I started to write this final chapter, I found myself gazing at the blinking cursor on the computer screen, uncertain about how to approach the closure to this journey through the realm of the five messengers. After many unproductive minutes, I decided simply to practice what I had been preaching in each chapter, and I paused to reflect upon the feelings that were accompanying the process of saying good-bye to the project and to you, the reader. What I became aware of was that all the messengers were a part of this ending, just as they had been throughout the writing of this book.

The vigilant triad as well as the desired duo visited me as I wrote the manuscript and its conclusion. Anger appeared every time I struggled to find the right word or experienced the annoyance of an unsatisfying sentence. Sadness came with the awareness that I would no longer have the book as a faithful presence in my daily routine. Fear surfaced as I considered the uncertainty about how this book will be received. Happiness came because I have been able to give form to the concepts and ideas I have been thinking about for a very long time, and I was likewise happy that my completed manuscript would now be on its way to the publisher. Love arrived when I thought about the many people who had inspired and supported this project.

Individually, these messengers informed me of the different emotional realities that are part of the ending process. Collectively, they led me to the conclusion that finishing this chapter was in my best interest, and I have steadfastly remained committed to making choices that would allow me to see this project through to the end. I am certain that all the messengers were also involved in the countless other experiences associated with writing this book, but these are the messages I was aware of in this moment of reflection. Few things are sweeter or more difficult than a good good-bye, and taking the time to consider the presence of the messengers made the bittersweetness of writing this closing chapter more personally meaningful and inspired me to press on.

I hope the reader will forgive me this moment of self-indulgence, but perhaps my intention is as obvious as I would like it to be. One of the fundamental premises of this book has been the notion that our feelings are our constant companions and are always available to add dimension and richness to our lives. Ironically, the discomfort that accompanies difficult or stressful life experiences often compels us to seek quick refuge without considering the true value of the associated feelings and the wisdom and guidance they offer. Though our feelings are always with us, unless we take the time to consider them, we may never be fully aware of their presence. Fortunately, it is also true that when we make a sincere effort to appreciate our emotional connection to the world around us, the presence of the five messengers is immediately apparent.

LIVING THE AUTHENTIC LIFE

I did not intend for this book to be the definitive treatise on feelings. I am well aware that there are many other physiological, psychological, and philosophical perspectives on human emotion. I have presented the feelings as five messengers, representing what I believe to be the essential components that make up all emotional experience. I am certain this concept of a quintet of elemental emotions could be subject to debate; I am just as certain other constructs could have their own merit. Ultimately, it makes no difference whether feelings can be distilled to five or six or twenty basic parts; these arbitrary, discrete categories merely provide a structure for describing the truly important thing— emotional experience.

While emotional experience is the basic meeting point of perception and sensation, however, it does not in itself guarantee any satisfaction or internal peace. It is only through *awareness* of our emotional experiences that we can begin to appreciate the ways feelings can inform and guide us. The desire and willingness to follow the guidance that flows from emotional awareness is the pathway to peace of mind.

The notion of the five messengers has been offered as a construct for considering our relationships with our own feelings, which is the basis of emotional awareness. I have tried to present feelings as normal, human responses to life experiences, and I have attempted to instill in the reader an appreciation of all feelings—from the most pleasant emotional sensations to the most difficult and unpleasant emotional experiences—as valuable messengers and guides. It is my firm belief that a judgment-free regard for feelings permits honest self-exploration and is a crucial element in self-acceptance.

It is normal and healthy to strive for self-improvement and self-actualization, and in this regard, each person's journey is unique. In the end, everyone faces the challenge of developing an authentic relationship with both the inside and the outside worlds. There can be no true authenticity without an honest acceptance of one's own feelings. Our emotional experience can be thought of as our sense of human *being*, and the matchless quality of each person's emotional life is the very essence of individuality. A healthy relationship with our feelings gives each of us the opportunity to appreciate the intricacies of our own uniqueness and offers us our emotional truth for consideration, guidance, and growth.

FRINGE BENEFITS

If a healthy relationship with our messengers only helped us find self-acceptance and peace of mind, that would be more than enough. But a good relationship with feelings offers us benefits in the interpersonal arena as well as within ourselves. A healthy appreciation of feelings leads not only to a greater regard for our own emotions but also a regard for the feelings of others. Mindful consideration of feelings paves the way for more respectful relationships and holds the promise of making us better parents, friends, and citizens.

Dr. Jacob Moreno, whom I mentioned in the chapter on happiness, once said, "A truly therapeutic procedure cannot have less an objective than the whole of mankind." This statement may seem like a grandiose notion of what therapy has to offer, but the spirit of Moreno's statement is simply this: the mental health of even one individual has an impact upon the other individuals in that person's life and, by extension, has an impact upon the whole world. Emotional awareness is not, in itself, therapy, but as an effort at self-improvement, emotional awareness is certainly a therapeutic endeavor.

When we do what we can to develop and maintain a healthy relationship with the five messengers, we are investing in our own well-being and in the well-being of the relationships we will develop throughout our lives. Perhaps, in a small way, a healthy relationship with feelings can truly change the world. Changing

the world is a pretty tall order, though, and if this book has simply encouraged you to regard feelings in a new or renewed light,
I will consider my efforts duly rewarded.

THE BEACON AND THE ROAD MAP

The inspiration for this book came from observations I made
during my work with clients in therapy. I had begun to see how
so much of my clients' suffering was connected to misguided notions about what feelings are, which left them unable to trust
their own emotions. Time and again I have had the honor of
bearing witness to the wonderful transformation that clients go
through as they learn to regard feelings as important aspects of
their own true nature and begin to claim their right to their own
experience of life.

Outside the therapy room it is not hard to see that many
people are on very poor terms with their emotions and that misguided notions about feelings are a source of pain and suffering
for people in all walks of life. I began to think a lot about how
misconceptions and erroneous notions about feelings predispose
people to reject or avoid the very thing that makes us human,
and how disregard for feelings limits the ability to make truly informed choices.

My interest in writing this book started with these observations and thoughts, but the manuscript soon became a vehicle
for sharing many of my ideas about the nature of emotions and
the bountiful gifts they offer when we allow them to serve as
messengers and guides. It is my hope and wish that *The Wisdom
of the Five Messengers* has inspired you to appreciate the beauty and truth of the messages of anger, sadness, fear, happiness,
and love, which can be fully known only in the most personal
way. Ultimately, their messages are your wisdom, your beauty,
and your truth.

The five messengers are both a lighthouse beacon and a road
map. As a beacon, the messengers serve as a guiding light ema-

nating from a fixed point, always available to lead us back to our own true nature when the way is foggy. As a road map, the messengers are the instrument that shows us the way through life's emotionally challenging landscape and helps us chart a course of our own choosing. With a constant beacon and a reliable map to guide us, we can never be lost.

ACKNOWLEDGMENTS

The ideas presented in *The Wisdom of the Five Messengers* have evolved over many years of clinical experience. They have taken form as a result of numerous discussions with teachers, supervisors, colleagues, and friends, to whom I am deeply grateful. First and foremost, I am thankful to the many clients I have had the privilege of serving and from whom I have learned the most about the wise guidance of emotions.

This book would not have been possible without the encouragement and support of many people. I want to thank all of the following individuals for the special role each one played in bringing this book to life: Christine Courtois, Ph.D.; Esther Giller, Mary Lou Kenney, and the Sidran family; J. Lawrence Jamieson, Ph.D.; Linda O'Doughda; Janis Potter; and Norman E. Weitzberg, Ph.D.

I also want to thank the many colleagues who responded to my request and provided suggestions for the resource section of this book. I am honored to be part of such a wonderful community of healers. Many thanks to: Ellen K. Baker, Ph.D.; Linda Bianchi, LCSW; Tara Brach, Ph.D.; Monica Callahan, Ph.D.; Cathi Cohen, LCSW; Michael Diamond, M.D.; Lisa Diamond-Raab, M.A., LPC; Jennell Evans, M.A.; John Gualtieri, Ph.D.; Milton Hawkins, LICSW; Peggy Heller, Ph.D., LICSW, RPT; Wendi Kaplan, LCSW; Kirsten M. Lundeberg, LPC, LMFT; Theresa Marks, M.A., ATR; Gloria Mog, LCSW; Pamela Oakley-Whiting, CNS-PMH, FNP-C; Ira Orchin, Ph.D.; Barry Spodak, LICSW; Marsha Stein, LCSW; David F. Swink, M.A., LICSW; Kathryn Viewig, M.Ed., CEAP; and Michelle R. Ward, LPC, LMFT.

RESOURCES

In the process of putting together this list of resources, I reached out to members of my professional community for suggestions. I was touched by the number of thoughtful responses they provided, including many references that were new to me. The following list is composed largely of the recommendations of these colleagues and friends whose work and outlooks I admire. I offer these resources for readers who want to further explore some of the topics discussed in this book.

FEELINGS

Alberti, R., and M. Emmons. *Your Perfect Right: A Guide to Assertive Living.* Atascadero, CA: Impact Publishers, 2001.

Aliki. *Feelings.* New York: Harper Trophy, 1986

Burns, D. *Feeling Good: The New Mood Therapy.* New York: Avon Books, 1999.

Chodron, P. *When Things Fall Apart: Heart Advice for Difficult Times.* Boston: Shambhala Publications, Inc., 2002.

Cronkite, K. *On the Edge of Darkness.* New York: Doubleday, 1994.

Dalai Lama. *The Art of Happiness: A Handbook for Living.* New York: Riverhead Books, 1998.

de Becker, G. *The Gift of Fear.* New York: Dell Publishing, 1997.

Depressive and Related Affective Disorders Association: *www.drada.org.*

Foxman, P. *Dancing with Fear: Overcoming Anxiety in a World of Stress and Uncertainty.* Lanham, MD: Jason Aronson, 1999.

Gaylin, W. *Feelings.* New York: Ballantine Books, 1986.

Gender, R. *The Book of Qualities.* New York: Harper & Row, 1988.

Goldie, P. (ed.) *Understanding Emotions: Mind and Morals.* Aldershot, Hampshire, UK: Ashgate Publishing, 2002.

Goleman, D. *Emotional Intelligence.* New York: Bantam, 1995.

Guarneri, M. *The Heart Speaks: A Cardiologist Reveals the Secret Language of Healing.* New York: Touchstone Books, 2006.

LeDoux, J. *The Emotional Brain: The Mysterious Underpinnings of Emotional Life*. New York: Touchstone Books, 1996.

Lerner, H. *The Dance of Anger: A Woman's Guide to Changing the Patterns of Intimate Relationships*. New York: Harper & Row, 1985.

Lewis, C. S. *A Grief Observed*. San Francisco: Harper, 1989.

Lewis, T., F. Amini, and R. Lannon. *A General Theory of Love*. New York: Vintage, 2000.

National Institute for Mental Health: *http://www.nimh.nih.gov*.

Niven, D. *The 100 Simple Secrets of Happy People*. San Francisco: Harper, 2001.

O'Donohue, J. *Beauty: The Invisible Embrace*. New York: HarperCollins, 2004.

Plutchik, R. *Emotion: A Psychoevolutionary Synthesis*. New York: Harper-Collins, 1980.

Quindlen, A. *A Short Guide to a Happy Life*. New York: Random House, 2000.

Redfield, K. *An Unquiet Mind*. New York: Knopf, 1995.

Rosenberg, M. *Nonviolent Communication: A Language of Compassion*. Encinitas, CA: Puddledancer Press, 2003.

Ross, J. *Triumph over Fear*. New York: Bantam, 1994.

Seligman, M. *Authentic Happiness: Using the New Positive Psychology to Realize Your Full Potential for Lasting Fulfillment*. New York: The Free Press, 2002.

Thayer, R. *Calm Energy: How People Regulate Mood with Food and Exercise*. New York: Oxford University Press, 2001.

MEDITATION

Aitken, R. *Taking the Path of Zen*. New York: North Point Press, 1982.

Brach, T. *Radical Acceptance: Embracing Your Life with the Heart of a Buddha*. New York: Bantam, 2003.

Gunaratana, H. *Mindfulness in Plain English*. Somerville, MA: Wisdom Publications, 1991.

Kabat-Zinn, J. *Wherever You Go, There You Are: Mindfulness Meditation in Everyday Life*. New York: Hyperion, 1994.

Kornfield, J. *A Path with Heart: A Guide Through the Perils and Promises of Spiritual Life*. New York: Bantam Books, 1993.

LeShan, L. *How to Meditate*. New York: St. Martin's Press, 1987.

Murth, J. *The Three Questions*. New York: Scholastic Press, 2002.

Nhat Hanh, T. *The Miracle of Mindfulness*. Boston: Beacon Press, 1999.

PARENTING AND CHILD DEVELOPMENT

Bang, M. *When Sophie Gets Really, Really Angry.* New York: Blue Sky Press, 1999.

Cohen, C. *Raise Your Child's Social IQ: Stepping Stones to People Skills for Kids.* Altamonte Springs, FL: Advantage Books, 2000.

Faber, A., and E. Mazlish. *How to Talk So Kids Will Listen & Listen So Kids Will Talk.* New York: Avon, 1980.

Hanson, R., J. Hanson, and R. Pollycove. *Mother Nurture.* New York: Penguin Books, 2002.

Kabat-Zinn, M., and J. Kabat-Zinn. *Everyday Blessings: The Inner Work of Mindful Parenting.* New York: Hyperion, 1997.

Leftin, H. *The Family Contract: A Blueprint for Successful Parenting.* Visilia, CA: PIA Press, 1990.

Mogel, W. *The Blessing of a Skinned Knee: Using Jewish Teachings to Raise Self-Reliant Children.* New York: Penguin Books, 2001.

Moreno, J. L. "Spontaneity Theory of Child Development," in J. L. Moreno, *Psychodrama First Volume,* 4th edition. New York: Beacon House, Inc., 1972.

Phelan, T. *1-2-3 Magic.* Glen Ellyn, IL: Child Management, 1995.

Pipher, M. *Reviving Ophelia: Saving the Selves of Adolescent Girls.* New York: Ballantine Books, 1994.

Siegel, D., and M. Hartzell. *Parenting from the Inside Out: How a Deeper Self-Understanding Can Help You Raise Children Who Thrive.* New York: Tarcher/Putnam, 2003.

Silverstein, O., and B. Rashbaum. *The Courage to Raise Good Men.* New York: Penguin Books, 1992.

Taffel, R., and M. Blau. *Nurturing Good Children Now.* New York: St. Martin's Press, 1999.

————. *The Second Family.* New York: St. Martin's Press, 2001.

RELATIONSHIPS

Gottman, J., and N. Silver. *The Seven Principles for Making Marriage Work.* New York: Three Rivers Press, 2000.

Hendricks, K., and G. Hendricks. *The Conscious Heart: Seven Soul Choices That Create Your Relationship Destiny.* New York: Bantam, 1997.

Hendrix, H. *Getting the Love You Want.* New York: Henry Holt and Company, 1988.

Keirsey, D., and M. Bates. *Please Understand Me: Character and Temperament Types.* Del Mar, CA: Prometheus Nemesis Book Co., 1984.

Lerner, H. *The Dance of Intimacy: A Woman's Guide to Courageous Acts of Change in Key Relationships.* New York: HarperCollins, 1989.
Scarf, M. *Intimate Partners: Patterns in Love and Marriage.* New York: Ballantine Books, 1988.
Schnarch, D. *Passionate Marriage: Love, Sex, and Intimacy in Emotionally Committed Relationships.* New York: W. W. Norton and Company, 1997.

SELF-REFLECTION AND PERSONAL GROWTH

Adams, K. *Journal to the Self: Twenty-two Paths to Personal Growth.* New York: Warner Books, 1990.
———. *Mightier Than the Sword: The Journal as a Path to Men's Self Discovery.* New York: Warner Books, 1994.
———. *The Way of the Journal: A Journal Therapy Workbook for Healing.* Baltimore, MD: Sidran Press, 1993.
Blatner, A., and A. Blatner. *The Art of Play: Helping Adults Reclaim Imagination and Spontaneity.* New York: Brunner/Mazel, Inc., 1997.
Chavis, G., and L. Weisberger. *The Healing Fountain.* St. Cloud, MN: North Star Press, 2003.
Ciardi, J., and M. Williams. *How Does a Poem Mean.* Boston: Houghton Mifflin, 1975.
Creech, S. *Love That Dog.* New York: HarperCollins Children's Books, 2002.
Dalai Lama. *How to Practice: The Way to a Meaningful Life.* New York: Pocket Books, 2003.
DeSalvo, L. *Writing as a Way of Healing: How Telling Our Stories Transforms Our Lives.* New York: HarperCollins, 1999.
Donaldson, O. *Playing by Heart: The Vision and Practice of Belonging.* Deerfield Beach, FL: Health Communications, Inc., 1993.
Epstein, M. *Thoughts Without a Thinker: Psychotherapy from a Buddhist Perspective.* New York: Perseus Book Group, 2004.
Fox, J. *Poetic Medicine: The Healing Art of Poem-Making.* New York: Putnam, 1997.
Gold, M., and M. Scampini. *When Someone You Love Is in Therapy.* Alameda, CA: Hunter House, Inc., 1993.
Hirsch, E. *How to Read a Poem: And Fall in Love with Poetry.* Fort Washington, PA: Harvest Books, 2000.
Kowit, S. *In the Palm of Your Hand: The Poet's Portable Workshop.* Gardiner, ME: Tilbury House Publishers, 1995.
Kripalu Center for Yoga and Health: *www.kripalu.org.*

Milner, M. *Eternity's Sunrise: A Way of Keeping a Diary.* London: Virago Press, 1989.

Morris, J. *The Dream Workbook.* Boston: Little, Brown & Co., 1985.

Omega Institute for Holistic Studies, Inc.: *www.eomega.org.*

Oriah Mountain Dreamer: *www.oriahmountaindreamer.com.*

Perrella, L. *Artists' Journals and Sketchbooks: Exploring and Creating Personal Pages.* Gloucester, MA: Quarry Books, 2004.

Ranier, T. *The New Diary: How to Use a Journal for Self-Guidance and Expanded Creativity.* Los Angeles: J. P. Tarcher, 1978.

Reynolds, D. *Flowing Bridges, Quiet Waters.* Albany: State University of New York Press, 1989.

Sark. *Sark's New Creative Companion: Ways to Free Your Creative Spirit.* Berkeley, CA: Celestial Arts, 2005.

TRAUMA AND RECOVERY

Note: The Sidran Institute offers extensive resources on issues related to trauma and recovery. Interested readers are encouraged to browse the Sidran Institute's online catalog of books and audiovisual materials on their Web site at *www.sidran.org.*

Cohen, B., M. Barnes, and A. Rankin. *Managing Traumatic Stress Through Art: Drawing from the Center.* Baltimore, MD: Sidran Press, 1995.

Courtois, C. *Healing the Incest Wound: Adult Survivors in Therapy.* New York: W. W. Norton & Company, 1988.

Dayton, T. *Trauma and Addiction: Ending the Cycle of Pain Through Emotional Literacy.* Deerfield Beach, FL: Health Communications, Inc., 2000.

Herman, J. *Trauma and Recovery.* New York: Basic Books, 1992.

Levine, P., and A. Frederick. *Waking the Tiger: Healing Trauma.* Berkeley, CA: North Atlantic Books, 1997.

Matsakis, A. *I Can't Get Over It: A Handbook for Trauma Survivors.* Oakland, CA: New Harbinger Publications, Inc., 1996.

Nhat Hanh, T. *The Moon Bamboo.* Berkeley, CA: Parallax Press, 1989.

Rothschild, B. *The Body Remembers: The Psychophysiology of Trauma and Trauma Treatment.* New York: W. W. Norton & Company, 2000.

Schiraldi, G. *The Post-Traumatic Stress Disorder Sourcebook: A Guide to Healing, Recovery and Growth.* Lincolnwood, IL: Lowell House, 2000.

Wilkinson, T. *Persephone Returns: Victims, Heroes, and the Journey from the Underworld.* Berkeley, CA: Pagemill Press, 1996.

ABOUT SIDRAN INSTITUTE

Sidran Institute, a leader in traumatic stress education and resources, is a national nonprofit organization devoted to helping people understand, recover from, and treat traumatic stress and related issues. We teach survivors, family members, and service providers; we consult with agencies and governments; we publish books, training materials, and assessment tools; and provide informational resources to thousands of survivors and providers each year. Our education and advocacy promotes greater understanding of:

- The early recognition and treatment of trauma-related stress in children;
- The long-term effects of trauma on adults;
- The strategies leading to greatest success in self-help recovery for trauma survivors, and support by and for their families;
- The most successful clinical methods and practices for treatment of trauma victims;
- The public policy initiatives that respond best to the needs of trauma survivors.

PROGRAMS

SIDRAN'S RESOURCE CENTER & HELP DESK provides information resources at no cost to callers and e-mailers from around the English-speaking world. The information includes: names of trauma-experienced therapists, traumatic stress organizations, educational books and materials, conferences, trainings, and treatment facilities.

SIDRAN SPEAKERS, TRAINING & CONSULTATION SERVICES provides conference and keynote speakers, pre-designed and custom training, consultation, and technical assistance on all aspects of traumatic stress–related content, including:

- *Public Education and Consultation* to organizations, associations, and governmental agencies on a variety of trauma topics and public education strategies.

- *Agency Training,* including our popular *Risking Connection*® program, on trauma-related topics such as Trauma Symptom Management, Self-Care for Helpers, The Relationship between Trauma and Dangerous Behavior, and others. We will be glad to customize presentations for the specific needs of your agency or organization.

- *Survivor and Community Education* programming including how to start and maintain effective peer support groups, community networking for trauma support, self determination, successful selection of therapists, coping skills, and healing skills.

SIDRAN INSTITUTE PRESS publishes books and educational materials on traumatic stress and dissociative conditions. A recently published example is *Risking Connection in Faith Communities: A Book for Faith Leaders Supporting Trauma Survivors.* Some of our other titles include *Growing Beyond Survival: A Self-Help Toolkit for Managing Traumatic Stress* and *Back from the Front: Combat Trauma, Love, and the Family.*

SIDRAN PILOTS COLLABORATIVE PROJECTS that create integrated service systems for holistic support of trauma survivors. Sidran is proud of its record of collaboration with a diverse range of organizations.

For more information on any of these programs and projects, please contact us:

SIDRAN INSTITUTE
200 East Joppa Road, Suite 207, Baltimore, MD 21286
Phone: 410-825-8888 • Fax: 410-337-0747
E-mail: info@sidran.org • Website: *www.sidran.org*

PUBLICATIONS • RESOURCES • TRAINING
COLLABORATIVE PROJECTS

ABOUT THE AUTHOR

Kerry Paul Altman, Ph.D., is a clinical psychologist in private practice in Fairfax, Virginia. This is his first book.

ALSO AVAILABLE FROM
SIDRAN INSTITUTE PRESS

Back from the Front: Combat Trauma, Love, and the Family, Aphrodite Matsakis

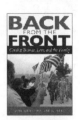

Ethics in Victim Services, Melissa Hook

Growing Beyond Survival: A Self-Help Toolkit for Managing Traumatic Stress, Elizabeth Vermilyea

Male Victims of Same-Sex Abuse: Addressing Their Sexual Response, John Preble and Nick Groth

Managing Traumatic Stress Through Art: Drawing from the Center, Barry Cohen et al.

Meeting at the Crossroads (VIDEO): Cross Training Between Mental Health and Sexual Assault Providers

Multiple Personality Disorder from the Inside Out, Barry Cohen, Esther Giller, and Lynn W., eds.

Restoring Hope and Trust: An Illustrated Guide to Mastering Trauma, Lisa Lewis, Kay Kelly, and Jon Allen

Risking Connection: A Training Curriculum for Working with Survivors of Childhood Abuse, Karen Saakvitne et al.

Risking Connection in Faith Communities: A Training Curriculum for Faith Leaders Supporting Trauma Survivors, Jackson Day et al.

Secondary Traumatic Stress: Self-Care Care Issues for Clinicians, Researchers, and Educators, B. Hudnall Stamm, ed.

Soldier's Heart: Survivor's Views of Combat Trauma, Sarah Hansel et al., ed.

Twenty-Four Carat Buddha and Other Fables: Stories of Self-Discovery, Maxine Harris

Unspeakable Truths and Happy Endings: Human Cruelty and the New Trauma Therapy, Rebecca Coffey

Vietnam Wives: Facing the Challenges of Life with Veterans Suffering Post Traumatic Stress, Aphrodite Matsakis

The Way of the Journal: A Journal Therapy Workbook for Healing, Kathleen Adams

FULL DESCRIPTIONS of these titles can be found at www.sidran.org. Order via the Website or call toll free 888-825-8249, ext. 210. Send inquiries to orders@sidran.org.